# SAILING'S
## STRANGEST®
# TALES

Other titles in the STRANGEST series

Cricket's Strangest Matches
Football's Strangest Matches
Golf's Strangest Rounds
Kent's Strangest Tales
Law's Strangest Cases
London's Strangest Tales
Medicine's Strangest Cases
Motor Racing's Strangest Races
Rugby's Strangest Matches
Running's Strangest Tales
Shakespeare's Strangest Tales
Teachers' Strangest Tales
Tennis's Strangest Matches


Titles coming soon

Cycling's Strangest Tales
Fishing's Strangest Tales
Horse Racing's Strangest Tales

# SAILING'S STRANGEST® TALES

Extraordinary but true tales from over
nine hundred years of sailing

## JOHN HARDING

**PORTICO**

Published in the United Kingdom in 2016 by
Portico
1 Gower Street
London
WC1E 6HD

An imprint of Pavilion Books Company Ltd

ISBN 978-1-91104-225-9

A CIP catalogue record for this book is available from the British Library.

10 9 8 7 6 5 4 3 2 1

Reproduction by Colourdepth UK
Printed and bound by Bookwell, Finland

This book can be ordered direct from the publisher at www.pavilionbooks.com

# CONTENTS

*I must go down to the seas again, to the lonely sea and the sky …'*

*(From 'Sea Fever',*
*by John Masefield)*

To the Kingarth Lads.

# INTRODUCTION

Whether sailing the Seven Seas in search of adventure, opportunities, unknown lands or to set new records of endurance, mankind has for centuries met with nautical triumph and disaster in almost equal measure. Powerful currents and feckless shipmates, unseen reefs and vengeful whales, monster waves and unimaginable storms, mysterious happenings and fateful miscalculations – all have plunged the unsuspecting sailor into desperate life-or-death struggles.

The strange stories generated by the sea and those who choose to sail upon it cover every emotion: desperate seamen are driven to eat a dead companion in order to survive; a round-the-world sailor is confronted with the ghost of Christopher Columbus, who guides him through a storm; and a young, newly-wed bride is forced to take command of a three-masted clipper ship when her husband falls perilously ill. These and a legion of other sailing tales that often defy logic are included in this fascinating book that will appeal to armchair sailors and salty sea dogs alike.

I first became entranced by the lure of the oceans when sailing to Australia as an emigrant in the 1950s. At naval school on the Isle of Wight I capsized a variety of dinghies and Flying Fifteens on the Solent before concluding that life ashore was a much safer bet.

**John Harding**

# A MEDIEVAL MURDER MYSTERY

## ENGLISH CHANNEL, 1120

On 25 November 1120, Henry I of England was preparing to set sail from the Norman port of Barfleur after the successful campaign of 1119, which had culminated in King Louis VI of France's defeat and humiliation at the Battle of Brémule.

Henry was approached by a young seafarer, Thomas FitzStephen. Thomas's father, Stephen, had been William the Conqueror's personal sea captain, taking him on the historic voyage of 1066 to fight against Harold, and he had ferried him back and forth across the Channel to the end of his life. Now his son Thomas had a newly fitted-out snakeship – the *White Ship* – of which he was particularly proud, and he offered it to the king for his voyage. Henry had already made his travelling arrangements, but he suggested it would be a treat for his son and heir, William, to sail on this state-of-the-art vessel. William was just 17 and a young man on whom many hopes rode.

As the rising star of the royal court, Prince William attracted the cream of society to surround him. He was to be accompanied by some 300 fellow passengers: 140 knights and 18 noblewomen; his half-brother and half-sister; and most of the heirs to the great estates of England and Normandy. There was a mood of celebration in the air and the prince had wine brought aboard ship by the barrel-load to help the party go with a swing. Both passengers and crew soon became highly intoxicated – shouting abuse at one another and ejecting a group of clerics who had arrived to bless the voyage.

The onboard revelries delayed the *White Ship*'s departure and it did not set out to sea until after night had fallen. The prince found that the king's fleet had already left him far behind, yet, as with all young rabble-rousers, he wished to be first back home. He therefore ordered the ship's master to have his oarsmen row full pelt and overtake them. Being as drunk as the rest of them, the master complied and the ship soon began to race through the waves.

An excellent vessel though the *White Ship* was, seafaring was not as safe as it is today. Many a boat was lost on the most routine of trips and people did not travel over the water unless they really had to. With a drunken crew in charge moreover, it seems that fate had marked out the *White Ship* for special treatment. It hit a rock in the gloom of the night and the port-side timbers cracked wide open, leaving a gaping hole.

Prince William's quick-thinking bodyguard immediately rushed him on deck and bundled him into a small dinghy. They were away to safety even before the crew had begun to make their abortive attempts to hook the vessel off the rocks. However, back aboard ship, the prince could hear his half-sister calling to him, begging him not to leave her to the ravages of the merciless sea. He ordered his little boat to turn round, but the situation was hopeless. As William grew nearer once more, the *White Ship* began to descend beneath the waves. More and more people were in the water now and they fought desperately for the safety of the royal dinghy. The turmoil and the weight were too much. The prince's little boat was capsized and sank without trace.

Finely dressed bodies, such as the Earl of Chester's, were washed up along the Norman shoreline for months after. It is said that the only person to survive the wreck to tell the tale was a Rouen butcher, called Berold, who had been on board only to collect debts owed him by the noble revellers!

But was it an accident, or was it political murder? Because Henry lost his only son and heir in the tragedy, a power vacuum of sufficient force was created to allow ambitious noblemen to become kingmakers and England's first civil war plunged the country into chaos. 'No ship ever brought so much misery to England,' wrote the chronicler, William of Malmesbury.

Intriguingly, one Stephen of Blois, a cousin of William's, *should* have been on the *White Ship* but, at the very last minute, claiming a sudden bout of stomach trouble, he boarded another craft. Four years later, he would seize the crown!

# HOW HIGH IS THE OCEAN, (HOW DEEP IS THE SKY)?
## ENGLAND, 1212

The English ancient historian Gervase of Tilbury in his work *Otia Imperiala* or 'Recreation for an Emperor', written around 1212 for his patron, the Holy Roman Emperor Otto IV, was adamant that 'the sea is higher than the land', that it was 'above our habitation ... either in or on the air.' Gervase was referring to a phrase from Genesis 1 in the Bible, which talks of 'waters above the firmament', but he also claimed hard evidence for this otherworldly concept. His research had discovered an event that occurred in an unnamed English village. As the parishioners were leaving church one morning following a service, they noticed a ship's anchor hooked onto one of the tombstones in the churchyard. What's more, on closer inspection it appeared that the anchor was attached to a rope that stretched upwards into the cloudy sky above. As the bemused congregation looked on, the rope began to sway and move about, just as if someone above was trying to unhook it. As the anchor remained stubbornly fixed, a figure – a 'sailor' according to Gervase – appeared as if from an unseen ship and proceeded to shin down the rope. This spectral deckhand quickly freed the anchor, but sadly for 'him' he wasn't quick enough to avoid being grabbed by one of the bystanders. Gervase concluded his tale:

He had already pulled the anchor free, when he was seized by the bystanders. He then expired in the hands of his captors, suffocated by the humidity of our dense air as if he were drowning at sea. The sailors up above wasted an hour, but then, concluding that their companion had drowned, they cut the rope and sailed away, leaving the anchor behind. And so in memory of this event it was fittingly decided that that anchor should be used to make ironwork for the church door, and it is still there for all to see.

# EUSTACE THE PIRATICAL MONK

## ENGLAND, 1217

Born in the late twelfth century, Eustace the Monk, sometimes known as the Black Monk, was a younger son of a lesser noble family in Boulogne and something of a Robin Hood figure. He was said to have a pact with the Devil, and the power to make his ship invisible, and sometimes disguised himself as a potter in order to confound his enemies. But Eustace was ultimately defeated in a sea battle in 1217 and had his head cut off!

As a young man he spent some time in a Benedictine monastery but was eventually outlawed and turned to piracy. Though the forces of Eustace were maritime in nature, his ships were little more than transport and floating battlefields, the primary strategy being to manoeuvre to board the enemy's ships and fight it out in a general mêlée.

Nevertheless, he and his followers soon came to control the Straits of Dover and, like many early pirates, he turned mercenary and sold the services of his ships and men to the highest bidder in 1205.

From 1205–12 he served King John of England in his war with Philip II of France, raiding the French coastline and seizing the Channel Islands – the island of Sark in particular – as a base of operations. Eventually, John outlawed Eustace for indiscriminate pillaging of English subjects, but soon forgave the pirate, as his services were too important.

However, Eustace and several other French buccaneers

switched sides in 1212. Serving the French, he attacked Folkestone to avenge the English seizure of his Channel Island bases. During the English civil war that broke out in 1215, he lent aid to the rebels and helped to transport and protect the troops of Prince Louis of France when they invaded southern England.

The war continued after King John died in 1216 and, with England in crisis, there was a rebellion by barons against the new young King Henry III. A French army was landed to support them. William the Marshal, the regent, conducted an effective campaign against them, recapturing coastal towns in Kent through which the French sent supplies.

Then a large French fleet set sail bound for London, a rebel stronghold, commanded by Eustace. Off the coast of Kent the French were intercepted by a British fleet under Hubert de Burgh, who sailed past the enemy and used the wind to blow his ships onto the rear of the French line.

A translated medieval poem (originally from *Li Romans de Witasse le Moine: Roman du Treizième Siècle*, published in 1972) recounts Eustace's final battle:

They defended themselves by throwing things and with lances and shooting with arrows. The French killed a lot of the English. They defended themselves like warriors. Eustace fought hard with an oar he held. He broke arms and legs. He killed this one and threw another down; he attacked another, and struck down a second, and crushed the third's throat, but they attacked him on all sides. The English worked hard at it and struck with great axes in the battle, but the French defended themselves so well that the English couldn't get on the ship. Then the English began to throw quicklime in great pots, that they hurled over the sides. The powder rose up in a big cloud. That was something that hurt them more; they couldn't defend themselves any longer, for their eyes were full of cinders. They were in the face of the wind, which tormented them.

The English then boarded and captured the French ships one by one. Several French nobles were later ransomed but, fearing that Eustace might pull off his famous vanishing trick, de Burgh beheaded him, there and then, on the quarter-deck of his ship!

# SHAKESPEARE'S TEMPESTUOUS *SEA VENTURE*

## BERMUDA, 1609

One of the best-known shipwrecks in literature is that of the merchantman *Sea Venture*, whose loss on a Bermudan reef in 1609 became the subject of William Shakespeare's play, *The Tempest*.

She was built in East Anglia in 1603, but her early history is not known with certainty. However, it is believed that she is the same *Sea Venture* owned by members of the Company of Merchant Adventurers, for whom she traded between London, the Elbe River port of Stade, and the Dutch market at Middleburg, carrying mostly wool and cloth.

In 1609 she was purchased by or chartered to the Virginia Company to sail as flagship of a supply mission sent out to the fledgling Jamestown colony established in 1607.

The ship sailed from Plymouth on 2 June with five other full-rigged ships and two pinnaces (small boats, often carried by larger vessels). On 23 July, a hurricane at sea separated the *Sea Venture* from the other vessels. After four days, when she began taking on water, the admiral of the flotilla, Sir George Somers, saw land.

Soon thereafter, the ship lodged between two reefs about three-quarters of a mile (1.2km) from land, and the entire company of 150 rowed ashore to Bermuda, a place dreaded by mariners who knew it as 'the Island of Devils'.

The ship remained afloat long enough for the crew to salvage most of her equipment and stores. The shipwrecked settlers quickly began planning their escape, however. Their mission, after all, was the rescue of Jamestown.

Although too damaged to be repaired, the *Sea Venture*, her rigging and planking supplemented by local red cedars, was refashioned in the following months into two smaller vessels, the *Deliverance* and the *Patience*, in which all but two of the company continued their passage to Jamestown, arriving on 10 May 1610.

In 1610, William Strachey, a member of the expedition, published an eyewitness account entitled *A True Repertory of the Wreck and Redemption of Sir Thomas Gates, Knight*, and Silvester Jourdain published *Discovery of the Bermudas otherwise called the 'Isle of Devils'*.

It is believed that Shakespeare read both of these accounts in the course of writing his romantic drama, *The Tempest* (1611), the last of his complete plays. There is little doubt that Shakespeare was privy to all documents pertaining to the expedition sponsored by his friends.

The opening scene of the play certainly shows Shakespeare's grasp of seamanship: 'Down with the top-mast; yare; lower, lower; bring her to try with main course!' Since books on this subject were not yet published, he probably got his information from working sailors as he describes the manoeuvres of the crew in the storm in precise nautical terms, exhibiting flawless seamanship.

The wreck of the *Sea Venture* remained undisturbed until 1959, when an American diver found it at a depth of 30ft (9.1m). Unfortunately, experts at the Tower of London misidentified one of the ship's guns as a saker dating from the eighteenth century, rather than a minion from the early seventeenth, and so work on the site ceased until 1978, when divers working under the auspices of the Bermuda Maritime Museum Association resumed operations.

# THE
# *FLYING DUTCHMAN*
## BERMUDA, CAPE OF GOOD HOPE, 1680–1959

The *Flying Dutchman* is, without a doubt, the best known of all ghost ships, although the term 'Flying Dutchman' actually refers to the captain, not his ship. The vessel, captained by Hendrick Van der Decken, set sail in 1680 from Amsterdam to Batavia, a port in Dutch East India (now North Jakarta, Indonesia). It encountered a severe storm as it was rounding the Cape of Good Hope but Van der Decken ignored the dangers – thought by the crew to be a warning from God – and pressed on.

Battered by the tempest, the ship foundered, sending all aboard to their deaths. As punishment, it was claimed, Van der Decken and his ship were doomed to ply the waters near the Cape for eternity. What's more, Van der Decken tries to pass letters home to other ships, but to accept these letters is certain doom.

The phantom ship has been seen many times – and there have been reports even in the twentieth century, including the crew of a German submarine during the Second World War.

One of the first sightings came in 1823, when a Captain W.F.W. Owen, a Royal Navy surveyor, recorded in the log of HMS *Leven* that a phantom ship was twice sighted, and on one occasion was seen to lower a boat to attempt communication. Captain Owen did not respond.

The captain and crew of another British ship in 1835

recorded that they saw the phantom ship approaching in the shroud of a terrible storm. It came so close that the British crew feared the two ships might collide, but then the ghost ship suddenly vanished.

In 1879, the steamer SS *Pretoria* changed course after the passengers and crew saw lights that they thought to be a distress signal. A strange sailing ship was seen, but it vanished when the steamer approached it.

The most famous Royal Navy sighting, however, was recorded by King George V, who in 1881 was a midshipman on HMS *Bacchante*. In his diary for 11 July, he unequivocally wrote 'At 4a.m., the Flying Dutchman crossed our bows.' The lookout on the forecastle and the officer of the watch also saw the ghost ship off the port bow. The then Prince George described 'a strange red light, as of a phantom ship, all aglow in the midst of which light the mast, spars and sails of a brig two hundred yards [183m] distant stood out in strong relief as she came up'. The ghost ship was sighted from other ships in the squadron, the *Cleopatra* and the *Tourmaline*. Thirteen crewmen, in all, witnessed the phenomenon. The squadron was commanded by Prince Louis of Battenberg, great-uncle of the present Prince Philip. The seaman who first reported the ghost ship died from a fall, only seven hours afterwards.

Coincidentally, in 1881, a Swedish merchantman under the command of Captain Larsen also encountered the *Flying Dutchman*. Captain Larsen's ship had been battling a storm as she rounded the Cape on her journey from Australia and shortly before dawn an eerie glow appeared in the sky. The captain sent a man up the mast to see what was the cause but he fell from his perch and crashed headlong onto the deck. He died several minutes later, having apparently whispered the words '*Flying Dutchman*'.

Another seaman went up the mast. The man, an Englishman called Landersbury, described a brilliant red flame in the middle of which there was an ancient vessel.

He could clearly see its mast, spars and sails and said that it was undoubtedly the *Flying Dutchman*. Two days before Captain Larsen's ship arrived at Rotterdam, Landersbury died of a heart attack. Another man, who had seen the manifestation through a porthole, was later discovered dead in his bunk and was said to have died of 'extreme fear'.

Three years later, in 1884, the American tea clipper *Relentless*, sailing for New York, also sighted the *Flying Dutchman* 300 miles (483km) south of the Cape of Good Hope. The captain, Daniel Sheaver, ordered the ship to alter course so that he could get a better look, but the helmsman died when they were 400 yards (366m) away from the phantom ship. That same night, a fierce gale hit the *Relentless* and three seamen were washed overboard and never seen again.

The next ship to claim a sighting was the Scottish whaling steamer, *Orkney Belle*, which encountered the *Flying Dutchman* in January 1911. The second mate described her giant sails swelling in a non-existent breeze. The *Orkney Belle* was so close to the *Flying Dutchman* that at one time it was thought that the two vessels must collide. As the *Flying Dutchman* sailed by, several of the *Orkney Belle*'s crew clearly saw her name on the stern. Three bells were heard from the phantom vessel, she heeled to starboard and vanished into the mist. In 1914 the *Orkney Belle* was one of the first British ships to be sunk in action by the German Navy on the outbreak of hostilities. Coincidence?

Not only sailors claimed to have seen the famous ghost ship. In March 1939, no fewer than 60 people at False Bay in South Africa had a complete view of the *Flying Dutchman* as she appeared to sail straight for the sands of Strandfontein. The *British South Africa Annual* of 1939 included the story, derived from newspaper reports:

With uncanny volition, the ship sailed steadily on as the Glencairn beachfolk stood about keenly discussing the whys and wherefores of the vessel. Just as the excitement reached its climax, however, the mystery ship vanished into thin air as strangely as it had come.

On a calm day in 1941, a crowd at Glencairn beach also saw a ship with wind-filled sails, but it, too, vanished just as it was about to crash onto the rocks while in September 1942, four people sitting on their balcony at Mouille Point, Cape Town, saw the same phantom vessel sail into Table Bay and disappear behind Robben Island.

The sightings continued on through the war. On 3 August 1942, HMS *Jubilee* was on the way to the Royal Navy base at Simonstown, near Cape Town. At 9p.m., a phantom sailing ship was seen. The second officer, Davies, was in charge of the watch. Sharing this duty was the third officer, Nicholas Monsarrat, author of *The Cruel Sea*. Monsarrat claims to have signalled to the strange ship, but there was no response.

Davies recorded in the log that a schooner, of a class that he did not recognise, was moving under full sail, even though there was no wind. The *Jubilee* had to change course, to avoid a collision. During the war, Davies's superiors would have been in no mood for nonsense, and he must have had to weigh that against the dangers, especially in wartime, of not recording the strange things that he saw. In an interview, Monsarrat admitted that the sighting inspired him to write his novel *The Master Mariner*.

Disasters associated with the ghost ship also continued. The escort boat, HMS *Beresford*, sailing westwards towards the Cape of Good Hope, broke radio silence to broadcast a two-worded message – '*Flying Dutchman*'. Then there was complete silence and neither the boat nor its crew of 34 men were ever seen again.

And, as recently as 1959, the Dutch freighter, *Straat Magelhaen*, captained by Captain P. Algra, came into contact with the *Flying Dutchman*. The ghostly vessel's sails were fully spread and a man could be seen clearly at the wheel. So sudden was the appearance of the ghostly ship that there was no chance of Captain Algra's taking avoiding action; but, just as the two vessels were about to collide, the *Flying Dutchman* vanished into the darkness.

Moan, ye Flying Dutchman, moan, for horrible is thy doom: The ocean round the stormy Cape it is thy living tomb.

# TWO GAY BUCCANEERS

## BAHAMAS, 1700s

Born in London, England, in the late seventeenth century, Mary Read was raised as a boy. Forced to support herself and her mother, she found a job as a footboy to a wealthy Frenchwoman living in London. Unhappy, she ran away and found employment aboard a man-of-war, but, after a few years of gruelling hardship and abuse, Mary jumped ship and joined the British military.

At first a lowly foot soldier, Mary showed true bravery at the Battle of Flanders and was soon promoted to the Horse Regiment. While in the Horse Regiment Mary became friends with another soldier, who believed her to be a man, but when she confessed her true gender the two married, bought out their commission in the military and opened an inn called the Three Horseshoes.

They prospered and were happy for a time, but when Mary's husband died she, once again, became a man. She left her inn and joined the military again, but soon hopped aboard a ship bound for the West Indies. While en route, the ship was attacked and captured by Captain Calico Jack Rackham and his pirate mistress, Anne Bonny.

Bonny had been born in Kinsale, Ireland, in the late 1690s, the daughter of respectable plantation owners in South Carolina. For young Anne, however, the rural comforts of plantation life were far less alluring than the stories floating around the nearby port of Charleston, a well-known pirate haunt. There, she met and married a small-time pirate named James Bonny, and the two moved to New Providence (now Nassau).

Pirates virtually ruled the city at that time. Surrounded by legendary figures such as Charles Vane and Calico Jack Rackham (the man who allegedly invented the skull-and-crossbones symbol), James Bonny had a difficult time commanding his wife's attention.

Anne soon left James for Rackham, joining the latter on his ship. Because the pirate code explicitly forbade female crew members, she disguised herself as a man and fought adeptly alongside the rest of the crew. It was only a matter of time before she was discovered, however, and, according to one legend, the first fellow shipmate to express anger at having a woman aboard paid for his opinion with his life. She stabbed him through the heart.

Bonny was now not the only female on board. She and Mary Read became fast friends. Suggestions that the two women were homosexual or at least bisexual is usually avoided by most 'pirate' historians but there was definitely a thriving gay subculture in New Providence. What's clear, however, is the two women's obvious enjoyment of cross-dressing, and the fact that they acted together as a couple and appeared to love one another.

Whether Rackham was jealous is also unknown. Whatever the state of their relationship, the trio happily wreaked havoc throughout the Caribbean for nearly a year until Bonny became pregnant. She gave birth in Cuba, then returned to the ship, apparently abandoning the child. Ironically, it would be another unwanted pregnancy that would later save her life.

In 1720, Rackham's ship was captured by one of Bahama's pirate-hunters. During the fight, Rackham apparently cowered in the hold along with most of the crew, while the two women stayed on deck and fought. After their capture, Rackham and the other men were hanged.

Bonny and Read were both pregnant, and thus escaped execution by 'pleading their bellies'. Read was sentenced to hang after giving birth, but before she could do so she died of a fever in jail. Somehow, Bonny was granted a reprieve, and what happened to her afterwards is entirely unknown. Some say she went back to her father or her husband; some say she resumed the pirate's life.

Whatever she did, her most memorable words are those she said to Calico Jack on the eve of his execution, quoted in Rictor Norton's *Lesbian Pirates: Anne Bonny and Mary Read*: 'I'm sorry to see you here, Jack, but if you'd have fought like a man you needn't hang like a dog.'

# THE GHOSTLY LADY OF GOODWIN SANDS

## GOODWIN SANDS, ENGLAND, 1748

At the point where the English Channel narrows to less than 20 miles (32.2km) lies a series of sandbanks known as the Goodwin Sands. Seafarers of all nations have for centuries lived in fear of this natural obstruction, whose infamous reputation is unrivalled anywhere in the world. Not surprisingly, perhaps, they have also been the cause of many legends, that of the *Lady Luvibond* being one of the most beguiling.

During the evening of 13 February 1748, the said schooner, loaded with a general cargo for Oporto, and under the command of Captain Simon Reed, sailed down the Thames to safely clear the North Foreland. It was a happy trip for Reed, with his new wife aboard, her mother and their wedding guests. However, Reed's first mate, John Rivers, had once hoped to marry Reed's new wife and was now consumed with hatred and jealousy.

As the guests drank toasts to the couple in the captain's cabin and a fair wind blew the *Lady Luvibond* across the water, something must have snapped in John Rivers's mind.

He drew a heavy wooden belaying pin from a rack, ambled towards the helmsmen and, pretending to peer over his shoulder at the binnacle, shattered the man's skull with the pin. Rolling the lifeless body aside, Rivers took the helm and swung the *Lady Luvibond* hard over until, with a grinding crash, the schooner hit the Goodwin Sands.

The masts snapped and toppled into the sea, and the timbers rent like matchwood. In the captain's cabin the bridal party had been too preoccupied to notice the ship's change of course, and were now trapped and helpless. Everyone, including the love-stricken Rivers, perished. By dawn on 14 February 1748, the *Lady Luvibond* had been sucked into the Goodwin Sands for ever.

Although there was evidence given at a subsequent court of inquiry to the effect that Rivers had vowed to get even with Simon Reed even if it cost him his life, the case of the *Lady Luvibond* was logged as misadventure.

It wasn't long before the compelling drama resurfaced in local folklore and it has become accepted that every 50 years, on the anniversary of the tragedy, the ship would come back and sail off the Kent coast as a ghost ship.

The belief was engendered when, 50 years later to the very day, a Captain James Westlake, aboard the coasting vessel *Eldridge*, was skirting the edge of Goodwin Sands when he caught sight of a three-masted schooner bearing down on him with sails set. Shouting to the helmsman to slam the wheel hard over, Westlake watched the other vessel veer past. As it did so, Westlake was sure he heard the sound of happy voices and merrymaking coming from the ship's lower decks.

Only when he reported the incident to the ship's owners did Westlake discover that the crew of a fishing vessel had seen the same schooner go ashore on the Goodwins, only to break up before their eyes. When they set out to rescue survivors, the crew of the fishing vessel found nothing but empty sand and water. The *Lady Luvibond*?

Thus the 50-year cycle began. On 13 February 1848, Deal fishermen watched the spectral *Lady Luvibond* go aground once more. They, too, were deceived by their own eyes and set out to rescue what they thought would be real people – but they, too, found nothing. And again, on 13 February 1898, watchers on the shore saw the *Lady Luvibond* re-enact yet again her fatal grounding and destruction on the Goodwin Sands. No trace of any tangible wreck was found.

Fittingly, there is now a local folk song dedicated to the passionate saga:

The captain's wife she looked above
And met the eyes of her ex-love
And all too late she recognised
The burning hatred in his eyes
His heart ablaze with jealousy
'If I can't have her, nor will he'
He spun the wheel out of his hands
And ploughed her on the dreaded
Goodwin Sands

And by the way, the *Lady*'s next appearance is scheduled for 13 February 2048.

# 'TOLL FOR THE BRAVE!'
## SPITHEAD, ENGLAND, 1782

The *Royal George* had been launched in 1756. At 2,047 tons, she was one of the largest ships of her day. She was just in time for the start of the Seven Years' War, during which she carried Admiral Edward Boscawen's flag in the Western Squadron on blockade service, and then the flag of Admiral Sir Edward Hawke when he virtually annihilated the French fleet at the Battle of Quiberon Bay.

In January 1781 she helped to escort a British convoy to Gibraltar and was among a group of ships capturing two weakly protected Spanish convoys. After this adventure she eventually returned to the Hamoaze for belated repairs. In October 1780, while she was in the Channel, the rudder had simply dropped off her stern. An admiral told an inquiry later that he had seen her opened up and had asked many questions. Her condition was so bad that he couldn't see one sound plank through the opening.

On 29 August 1782, she was at anchor at Spithead undergoing some minor repairs in preparation for an imminent voyage to the Mediterranean, where she was to be part of a naval force gathering to relieve Gibraltar. When the work started, not only the crew of about 880, but also some hundreds of visitors, family, friends and tradespeople were on board.

The vessel was heeled over to make repairs to a watercock. This was a makeshift method consisting of running the heavy guns from one side of the vessel to the other, requiring fine judgement to know just how far such a list could be sustained without endangering the ship's stability. A couple of hours after work started, a carpenter decided that things were starting to go wrong. After the officer of the watch ignored his appeal, he went to the commander, who ordered the cannon to be restored to their normal positions.

Everything seemed fine, but suddenly the vessel flooded with water; there was a heavy crack and the ship capsized and sank all within minutes.

As the depth of water was only about 90ft (27.4m), the top of the masts and part of the bowsprit could be clearly seen above the water, suggesting that the vessel had settled on the seabed on an even keel. People flocked to Portsmouth just to view the masts protruding above the water!

Incredibly, of the 880 officers and men, only 75 managed to escape. The captain, being unable to swim, was saved by some of his crew, but at a court martial later that year he was exonerated from all blame, the cause of the disaster being attributed to the decayed state of her timbers.

Over the years, various ingenious salvage attempts were made, including one by Alexander Siebe, demonstrating the efficacy of his new 'closed' diving suit – the now familiar diver's helmet incorporating an air-regulating outlet. But the Admiralty weren't overkeen to help, deciding, perhaps, that the evidence of their scandalous inefficiency was best left beneath the surface of the waves. Some 50 years later, divers did manage to bring up 29 bronze guns, which were later melted down and used in the base of Nelson's column. The ship's bell is now held by the National Maritime Museum.

The horror of the event inspired writers and painters alike. Captain Frederick Marryat, in his novel *Poor Jack*, would draw heavily on notes made by John Schetky, the famous marine painter, who in turn had received a vivid account from one of the survivors. Schetky's painting, *The Loss of the Royal George*, is now in the Tate Gallery, and the whole sorry affair was later immortalised in a poem by William Cowper, the first lines of which are:

Toll for the brave –
The brave! that are no more;
All sunk beneath the wave,
Fast by their native shore.

# 'I PUT A MESSAGE IN A BOTTLE ...'

## WORLDWIDE, 1784–1999

Messages placed in bottles have been known to float about for decades, even centuries. In sixteenth-century England, Queen Elizabeth I even appointed an official 'Uncorker of Ocean Bottles', making it a capital crime for any unauthorised person to open bottles found in the sea or washed up. The fear was that some might contain secret messages from spies, not to mention the British fleet, who used this unlikely method to send messages about enemy positions ashore.

The strangest – and most tragic – case of a message sent seeking help was perhaps that of Chunosuke Matsuyama, a Japanese seaman who was shipwrecked with 44 shipmates in 1784. Shortly before he and his companions died of starvation on a Pacific coral reef, Matsuyama carved a brief account of their plight on a piece of wood, sealed it in a bottle and then threw it into the sea. In 1935, 150 years later, it washed up – at the very seaside village where Matsuyama had been born.

Certainly one of the most poignant of such letters must be the one thrown by a passenger on board the torpedoed liner *Lusitania*, which sank in May 1915. According to one report, the message read, 'still on deck with a few people. The last boats have left. We are sinking fast. Some men near me are praying with a priest. The end is near. Maybe this note will–' Matching it for sadness, perhaps, was the one found in March 1999 by a fisherman in the Thames estuary. In 1914 while crossing the English Channel, a homesick British infantryman named Thomas Hughes wrote his wife a letter, sealed it in an empty ginger-beer bottle and tossed it overboard. Two days later, he perished in battle. The fisherman who found the note was flown to Auckland, New Zealand, and personally delivered the bottle to Hughes's 86-year-old daughter, who treasured it as the only letter she ever had from her father.

Not all messages found have such a bittersweet outcome, however. In 1948 a Russian fisherman found a message written in Norwegian and English. Once translated it made little sense: 'Five ponies and 150 dogs remain. Desire hay, fish and 30 sledges. Must return early in August. Baldwin.'

It transpires that the polar explorer Evelyn Baldwin sent it in 1902, and he had returned alive and well!

One day in 1956, Martin Douglas kissed his wife, Alice, goodbye and set off in his small cabin cruiser for a day of fishing off the coast of Florida near his home. When he didn't return on schedule, extensive air and sea searches swung into action. He was eventually, officially, declared 'missing at sea', and never seen again. About a year later, on an Australian beach, a jar was found with a note tightly sealed inside it.

Should this note be found, please forward it to my wife, Mrs. Alice Douglas, at Miami Beach, Florida. No doubt you're wondering what has became of me. I got blown out into the waters, due to engine trouble.

With the note was a blank cheque, on the back of which was the handwritten will of Martin Douglas.

But let's end things on a happy note. Paolina and Ake Viking were married in Sicily in the autumn of 1958, thanks to a far-travelling bottle. Two years earlier, Ake, a bored young Swedish sailor on a ship out at sea, had dropped a bottle overboard with a message asking any pretty girl who found it to write to him. Paolina's father, a Sicilian fisherman, picked it up and passed it to his daughter for a joke. Continuing the joke, Paolina sent off a note to the young sailor. The correspondence quickly grew warmer, Ake visited Sicily, and marriage soon followed.

# CAPTAIN BLIGH'S AMAZING JOURNEY

## TAHITI, 1789

The *Bethia* was built in Hull, England, as a coal-carrying merchant ship operating on the coast of England. In 1787, the Royal Navy purchased her and renamed her the *Bounty*, keeping the name 'Bethia' for the figurehead. Recommissioned for a special voyage, she was to sail halfway around the world to Tahiti, collect sapling breadfruit trees and transport them to the West Indies. Owners of the burgeoning British plantations there needed a cheap source of food for the workers.

To lead the mission, the Admiralty picked 33-year-old Lieutenant William Bligh, who had been the sailing master on the HMS *Resolution*, on Captain Cook's last voyage of discovery. Though portrayed as an abusive tyrant by Hollywood, Bligh may have been one of the greatest seamen who ever lived. After the HMS *Bounty* left England, she weathered a storm and all of her supplies were washed overboard. She stopped to resupply at Tenerife in the Canary Islands. After trying for 30 days to make it westward around Cape Horn, as he had been ordered, Bligh turned about and headed east, around the Cape of Good Hope, across the whole width of the Indian Ocean, then northeast into the Pacific, arriving in Tahiti after a ten-month voyage.

There, Bligh and the crew set about collecting the more than 1,000 breadfruit plants they were to take to the Caribbean. They spent five months in Tahiti, during which time Bligh allowed a number of the crew to live ashore, to care for the potted breadfruit plants. Without the discipline and rigid schedule of the sea, the men went native. Three crewmen deserted, hoping to spend their days in this tropical paradise, but were recaptured by Bligh and flogged.

Three weeks out of Tahiti, en route to the West Indies with the breadfruit plants, Master's Mate (Acting Lieutenant) Fletcher Christian, angered and humiliated over the continual abuse from Captain Bligh, took the ship. Of the 44 men on board the HMS *Bounty* during its ill-fated voyage, 31 sided with Bligh on that fateful 28 April 1789.

At dawn that day, Captain William Bligh and 18 men from HMS *Bounty* were herded onto a 23ft (7m) launch and abandoned in the middle of the Pacific Ocean.

The mutineers, numbering about half of the remaining 25 crewmen, but in command of the *Bounty* having secured all the firearms aboard, sailed the ship to the island of Tubuai. After an unsuccessful three-month effort to settle on the island, they returned to Tahiti, put 16 of the crew ashore, some loyal to Bligh, some mutineers. Fletcher Christian and eight *Bounty* crew, accompanied by six Tahitian men and 12 women, one with a baby, sailed away in the *Bounty* hoping to hide for ever from the long arm of the British law. They eventually settled on Pitcairn Island, an isolated rock in the Pacific that was misplaced on British charts. They burned the ship in what is now called Bounty Bay and weren't discovered for 18 years.

Bligh, meanwhile, had set out on an extraordinary journey, probably one of the greatest achievements in the history of European seafaring and a personal triumph for a man who has been misjudged by history.

Having no charts, he navigated the launch nearly 4,200 nautical miles (7,778km) to safety in 41 days using only a sextant and a pocket watch. Only one man died on the voyage – stoned to death by angry natives on the first island they tried to land on. The launch voyage was a feat of navigation unparalleled to this day. Navigating by the stars, bailing frantically as storms filled the tiny vessel with water, they were forced to eat the foulest stuff imaginable, such as half-digested flying fish and squid discovered in the stomach of a seabird that had been foolish enough to perch on the edge of the boat.

All the while Bligh obsessively (if not dutifully) made notations and drawings of landforms along the way. It is an incomparable achievement, yet, on his return to England, it would be questions of the mutiny that dominated the headlines, all but obscuring this tale of brilliant navigation and survival.

# A *CONSTELLATION* OF GHOSTS

## USA, 1797–1999

The original *Constellation* was built as a 36-gun frigate, and launched from Harris Creek, Maryland, USA, on 7 September 1797 – and there cannot be quite another ship so beset with ghosts as this one. Commodore Thomas Truxton was her first captain and he got her career off to a bloody start.

In 1799, after a major sea victory against the French in the West Indies, it was discovered that seaman Neil Harvey had fallen asleep while on watch. Truxton first ordered a lieutenant to stick him with his sword. Wounded, but still alive, Harvey was then executed in the traditionally brutal way: tied in front of a cannon and blown to bits.

Neil Harvey has become one of the most frequently seen ghosts seen aboard the *Constellation*, apparently appearing as a shimmering mass, mainly, it's said, because that is the way he sees himself after being blown up.

Captain Thomas Truxton himself has also been seen – so often, in fact, that in December 1955 a Lieutenant Commander Allen R. Brougham set out to investigate the persistent stories. He called a photographer friend and asked him to come aboard one night with his camera. They set up on a spot overlooking the ship's wheel. Very close to midnight, the figure of a nineteenth-century US Navy captain appeared and was captured on film. 'It was all over within the time he took to make a single stride,' Brougham told a reporter. The stunning photograph, described as having a 'bluish white radiancy', appeared in a local paper a few days later. It shows a man in gold epaulettes bending over slightly, reaching across his waist with his right hand as if to draw his sword.

Another prevalent spirit is said to be that of an 11-year-old boy, the surgeon's assistant aboard the USS *Constellation* in the 1820s, who was murdered by two other sailors with a knife in the cockpit of the orlop (storage) deck. Another is of a sailor who had become overwhelmed with the awful conditions on board, and hanged himself. He's described as a sad entity who likes to float around and across the gun and forecastle decks.

The *Constellation* was eventually reconstructed in 1845 and some believe that the entire 1797 vessel was scrapped and a completely new ship was erected. Other analysis has proved that timbers, materials and equipment were used from the original ship. Whatever was left of the original vessel, its use in the new ship was enough to keep the ghosts around. In time, when she had outlived her uses, money was raised to take her back to Baltimore, where she arrived in September 1955 and was docked at a local shipyard to await repairs. This is when stories of ghosts began to surface.

Sailors standing night watch on nearby ships reported odd noises and unidentifiable shapes. The submarine *Pike* was moored closest to the *Constellation* and the submariners frequently saw ghosts walking on the old warship. People reported smelling gun smoke before the appearance of some apparitions, especially of Captain Truxton.

Not all the ghosts are miserable, however. Carl Hansen, a mid-twentieth-century night-watchman, is believed to be the only spirit that is actually happy aboard the ship. He cared for the *Constellation* until an alarm system was installed in 1963 and his spirit has been seen playing cards on the lower decks. He adored the ship, and had a strong emotional bond with it. In his younger days, he was a Royal Navy cook, making him an old sailor himself. At a Sea Scouts' Hallowe'en party, his ghost apparently sat next to a young girl and smiled at her. One day a priest came aboard the ship and was given a tour by an enthusiastic and knowledgeable guide. Before he left he praised the man's services to the staff. The guide didn't fit the description of anyone working there – but it did fit Carl Hansen. The *Constellation* most recently came back from dry dock on 2 July 1999 and on 26 October 2004, she made her first trip out of Baltimore's Inner Harbour since 1955. The trip to the US Naval Academy in Annapolis lasted six days, and marked her first trip to Annapolis in 111 years.

Apparently, however, the spirits are still aboard. Late one evening a night-watchman was inspecting the ship's storage deck. It was late and he had only a flashlight to lead him through this narrow area at the bottom of the ship. A misty white light appeared out of nowhere and became a sailor in an outdated uniform. He walked towards the watchman. The man stood still as the ghost passed through him.

# WILLIAM WORDSWORTH'S DEEP DISTRESS

## SHAMBLE'S BANK, ENGLAND, 1804

The poet William Wordsworth was very close to his youngest brother, John, a sailing captain. They spent time together at Dove Cottage, Grasmere, the home of William and their sister Dorothy, and John hoped to buy himself some property there and support William while the latter devoted himself to his poetry.

John's present ship, the *Earl of Abergavenny*, was a large East Indiaman of over 1,180 tons. She was built in 1789 and, by 1804, John had safely captained seven voyages to the Far East. John had lobbied the East India Company to obtain the command of such a ship on the London–Bengal–Canton route because this would enable him to buy opium in Bengal to sell at a handsome profit in Canton. The trade in opium was then sanctioned by the enthusiastic connivance of British and Chinese officials alike and in Britain opium was sold without legal control and regarded as a medicine or, at worst, a personal indulgence.

For the coming voyage he had invested about £20,000 in such goods, including £1,200 belonging to William and Dorothy.

The *Abergavenny* left Portsmouth on 5 February 1804 along with three other ships guided by a naval frigate, HMS *Weymouth*. She was carrying more than 400 passengers.

By mid-afternoon on the same day some very heavy winds blew up. As they passed through the Needles Channel, the ship became stranded on the nearby Shambles Bank.

This did not give cause for concern and no distress signals were fired. John waited for the tide to turn, so refloating the ship.

An hour and a half later, when they were on their way, it became obvious that they had sustained a large leak and water was gushing into the hold. John was still relatively unperturbed and he prepared to return to Portsmouth.

As he did so, even stronger winds prevailed and the first mate reported 12ft (3.7m) of water in the hold. The level was rising all the time because the pumps could not cope.

Crewmen launched one of the ship's boats and set off to try to prevent further damage to the hull; they all drowned. No further boats were launched and at 9p.m. that evening John informed the passengers of the gravity of their situation.

At about 11p.m. the vessel gave 'a sudden lurch' and within minutes it had sunk on an even keel in some 60ft (18.3m) of water. This left some of the shrouds and about 25ft (7.6m) of the main mast proud of the water, where passengers, crew and troops clung for dear life, but very few survived for long in the intense cold and piercing high winds.

Other vessels tried to come to their rescue but couldn't get near enough except for a large sloop, which managed to save about 60 people.

John Wordsworth's body was washed ashore near Weymouth over a month later. He had last been seen clinging to the mast, resolutely refusing to leave his ship.

He was buried in a mass grave with almost a hundred others in Wyke Regis churchyard.

To add insult to injury, particularly for the Wordsworth family, John was rumoured to have been completely responsible for the tragedy and had given his own life on purpose out of a sense of shame and disgrace.

An exhaustive investigation was made by the English essayist Charles Lamb, a close literary friend of William's.

He was able to conclude that John had acted absolutely according to his professional code of practice.

The drowning of John gave Wordsworth the strongest shock he had ever experienced. So affected was he that, for three months, he stopped work on *The Prelude* and the powerful lines from his gospel of Nature, 'Elegiac Stanzas Suggested by a Picture of Peele Castle'. 'A deep distress hath humanised my Soul,' he lamented.

John's ceremonial sword was recovered from the wreck and presented to William. It is still in the possession of the family.

# DYING FOR A BITE
## ENGLISH CHANNEL, 1826

On 8 May 1826 the brig *General Brock* left Jersey. The weather was agreeable until the 29 May, when around half past midnight, visibility was obscured by a thick mist. The crew then saw a ship coming towards them at great speed and, despite their doing everything possible to avoid her, she ran into them on their starboard bow, smashing it to pieces. The ships were entangled for about five minutes and four of the crew ended up on the other ship. In trying to take on crew members from the *Brock*, the mystery ship suddenly found the wind behind it and in an instant it was lost from sight.

Seeing that the *Brock* was rapidly going under, 14 crew clambered into a small boat, having had to leave one man behind in the hold because he didn't have the time to come on deck.

As soon as they were clear of the ship, it sank, leaving the 14 in a little boat with neither bread nor water, nor indeed any provisions except a small Dutch cheese. In the boat were two oars, a compass, a lantern and light and a foghorn.

They rowed towards where they hoped to find the ship that had sunk them, but it was in vain. Towards six o'clock in the morning they decided to row for land. At first the weather was agreeable, though very cold. Soon, however, hunger and thirst began to take their toll. By 11 in the morning of the next day, the wind rose and the sea became rough. The night passed with a strong breeze and on the third day strong winds blew them to the north, and the cold penetrated because of their lack of clothing.

On the fifth day at about six o'clock in the evening, having no strength, they had finished rowing when they saw a ship about 2 miles (3.2km) to windward heading east. Revived, they gave everything they had to row for this ship, shouting, making signals with handkerchiefs and scarves tied to an oar, but they were not seen.

They resigned themselves to their fate, deprived of all hope. One of the crew, Joseph Powell, later wrote an account of what happened next:

One of our fellow creatures was on his last legs and it pleased God to redeem him around 10 o'clock. The next morning about 8 o'clock we were looking at our poor dead brother, talking about throwing him in to the sea. A young boy, at that moment tormented by the great pains of hunger and thirst, suggested that he had heard that in some such occasions similar to ours that there had been some people who had eaten the flesh of the corpses. He asked if he would be permitted to satisfy his craving on this occasion – nobody opposed this.

He then took a small hatchet and cut the two thighs of this poor unfortunate. He ate some of it himself and then gave some of it to everyone else. We ate some of it – ever so little – crying and looking at each other …

Despite the resort to cannibalism, the weaker men died – six in the last six days. On 9 June, the four crewmen who managed to survive the ordeal were picked up by the brig *Ann* of Liverpool.

# THE *QUIXOTE*

## ATLANTIC OCEAN, 1831

The *Quixote* was a 120-ton brig, built in New Brunswick in 1828 and owned by Pierre Duval of St Aubin. In the summer of 1830 with Francis Bailhache as master, she sailed for Newfoundland, thence to Cadiz and then to San Lucar in Spain, where she took on a cargo of oil for Liverpool.

She left on 23 October and ran into incessant storms until 5 December, when it reached hurricane force, obliging them to heave to. She was attempting to scud under main topsail when, at 6.30p.m., the brig was struck amidships by a tremendous sea and thrown onto her beam ends, causing the cargo to shift.

On deck, the two-man watch cut away the lanyards of the rigging, the masts went over the side and the vessel righted herself, but she was full of water because the hatches had been smashed in. When the sea struck, four men had been in the fore cuddy but three drowned. The master and the mate managed to make their way from the aft cabin to the deck, where they saw the seas sweeping the deck from stem to stern.

The remainder of the crew, completely drenched and nearly exhausted, held on despite the intense cold. Two hours after the knock-down, the master died, and the following morning another of the crew died, worn out by cold and fatigue. The four survivors clung on to the wreck for the next four days with neither food nor drink.

On 9 December another crewman died and the remaining men lashed his body to prevent it being washed away – in order that they might feed on it. The following day, 10 December, they gnawed at an arm, and on 11 December they gnawed some more. On 12 December, the storm was abating but the body was becoming putrid. On the morning of 13 December, Philip Arthur saw a sail and was able to signal it.

The French brig *Ceres of Rouen*, bound for Harfleur, took them on board but one of the survivors died, leaving Clement Noel, the mate, and Philip Arthur, both Jersey men, the only survivors. They were landed at Harfleur where they were placed in hospital and where they stayed for 17 days after which they travelled to Havre-de-Grace (Le Havre) by steamship.

When the crew were rescued by the Frenchmen, the *Quixote* was left as a drifting hulk. She was spotted by Captain Walker of the *Susannah* on 19 December, by which time she had lost half her mainmast and the foremast had gone completely.

Three months later she was salvaged by Spanish fishing boats, which found her drifting, She was towed into the port of Santander on 19 March 1831, minus her masts but with her cargo still in good condition.

# AMAZING GRACE

## NORTHUMBERLAND, ENGLAND, 1838

The Longstone Lighthouse on the Farne Islands, off Northumberland, contained four rooms below the lantern, where William Darling and his wife lived with their nine children. All of the family, except Grace and her brother William, left home in due course, but these two regularly looked after the light.

In the early hours of 7 September 1838, William was ashore when Grace saw the paddle steamer *Forfarshire* grounded on a rock. Of the 60 people on board, only a dozen or so remained alive and managed to scramble onto the rocks.

During the night two children and two more adults died from exposure and their injuries. Then, at daybreak, Grace and her father rowed out to the wreck in the lighthouse coble (a short, flat-bottomed boat). Grace and her father were able rowers, but the violent tide pushed the stout little boat off course several times, making their journey to the *Forfarshire* twice as long. They reached the wreck and took off five of the nine survivors, who were taken back to the lighthouse.

Grace stayed with those rescued while her father and two of the rescued seamen made a second trip to the wreck to fetch the remaining survivors. When the rescued were safely inside the lighthouse, Grace and her mother tended to injuries and cooked meals. It was three days before the survivors could be taken ashore.

On 11 September newspapers of the day printed the story

of the loss of the *Forfarshire*. There was no mention of the Darlings' bravery, as arguments over the cause of the wreck and the possibility that the *Forfarshire*'s owners had wilfully sent a disabled ship to sea eclipsed the news of the rescue. When the scandal died down, a 'penny-a-liner' reporter grabbed the Grace Darling story for his gossip sheet and gave it his melodramatic best. The deed leaped from paper to paper, with each account more thrilling and courageous.

The rescue, and Grace in particular, suddenly became something of a legend and her part in the drama became one of the most celebrated cases of female heroism of the Victorian era. Painters rushed to Longstone to capture Grace's dainty face and slight figure against a backdrop of angry seas and suffering humanity. Poets wrote tributes to the 'Grace of womanhood and Darling of mankind', and peddlers hawked locks of her hair and swatches of fabric from the dress she had worn on the rescue. Boat trips were organised to the Longstone Lighthouse for people just to get a glimpse of her. A public conscription for the Darlings raised a gift of several hundred pounds, to which the Royal Humane Society added gold lifesaving medals and a silver tea set.

She continued to live on Longstone Lighthouse with her parents, but was besieged with mail, visitors and requests for appearances. She went ashore to Bamburgh in April 1842 to visit her sister and attend to financial affairs, but was stricken with influenza; Grace never recovered.

In October 1842, four years after her brave accomplishment, Grace died, probably of pneumonia – a tragic finale that caused much public grief and elevated her image to saintly eminence. She was buried in Bamburgh churchyard before a huge crowd of mourners, who also contributed money for a memorial to be built over her grave. Even Queen Victoria sent £20. St Aidan's Church had a stained-glass window made showing Grace rescuing the shipwrecked. A little museum in the village still displays the original coble; it is in the care of the Royal National Lifeboat Institution.

# POWER AND THE
# *PRESIDENT*

## ENGLAND, 1841

In 1841 the grandfather of the great twentieth-century film star Tyrone Power, an actor himself, and of the same name, proposed a trip to England. He wanted to visit an old friend, Benjamin Webster, who owned the Haymarket Theatre in London. He was one of the 121 passengers on the *President*, the largest steamship afloat at that time, propelled by means of paddlewheels and sails.

This was to be an impressively fast crossing: New York to London in 16 days! She left New York on 11 March. On 13 March, far away in Blackheath, London, a violent storm raged during the night. Ben Webster's terrified manservant awoke his master to tell him that a Mr Tyrone Power had been knocking on the front door, shouting that he was 'drowned in the rain'.

Webster dashed out into the darkness and found nothing. The *President* never arrived in Liverpool. She vanished on 11 March 1841 without a trace, along with her crew and passengers – including the 'drowning' Tyrone Power.

# HARD RATIONS:
# DEATH IN THE ARCTIC
## CANADA, 1846

The explorer Sir John Franklin set out on his fourth search of the Northwest Passage on 19 May 1845, with 134 sailors and officers in two vessels, the *Erebus* and *Terror*. With five years of food supplies, including eight thousand tins of meat, vegetables and soup, they were better equipped than any previous polar expedition.

Both ships carried impressive libraries totalling around three thousand volumes on various subjects. Both were heated by hot water running in pipes under the floors of the berths. Both held schooling classes for the less educated members of the crews. Perhaps most impressive of all was that both the *Erebus* and *Terror* had entire locomotives, weighing 15 tons each, installed in their holds. Acquired from London Railways, these massive 20-horsepower engines were specially adapted to move the ships through broken ice floes.

The two ships were last seen at the end of July that year by the crew of two whaling ships, who sighted Franklin's expedition tied to massive ice floats. Two years on, and with no contact having been established, the British Admiralty commissioned three expeditions to seek Franklin and offer relief. They returned to England after failing to find a trace of either ships or crews. Rewards were offered for information leading to their discovery and rescue.

On 23 August 1850, HMS *Assistance* finally found traces

of the expedition at Cape Riley, Devon Island: three graves, side by side, dug into the permafrost, complete with carved wooden headstones that bore the date 1846.

Almost a decade later, on 25 May 1859, a party of Arctic explorers came across a complete skeleton, still dressed in a steward's uniform. A notebook and comb were lying alongside the remains, revealing that its owner had been a petty officer on HMS *Terror*.

Days later, a lifeboat littered with clothing, weapons and skeletons was discovered. What puzzled the explorers was the astonishing array of needless articles such as books, slippers, toothbrushes, silk cloth, combs, boots, vast amounts of soap and many other items found aboard, while the only food remaining was chocolate and tea! An already exhausted party must have found the extra weight in this mountain of luxuries an unnecessary burden.

Further searches uncovered more remains, some of which bore the tell-tale evidence of cannibalism, a theory backed up by native Inuit stories. In fact, only a small proportion of the 129 men's remains were ever found.

Reports of ghostly ships floating in the icy waters have cropped up in the years since the tragedy. One such sighting, by air in 1937, reported a massive bulk lying motionless on top of a huge iceberg, but, after returning home to refuel, the pilot was unable to relocate either the ship or the floating ice mass. But these perhaps inevitable tales pale before the banality of the explanation as to just what went so drastically wrong with the Franklin expedition.

Forensic evidence taken from the bodies in the graves at Devon Island and painstaking research of the numerous artefacts found littering the Arctic ice has suggested that a combination of cold, starvation and disease including scurvy, pneumonia and tuberculosis, all made worse by lead poisoning, killed everyone in the Franklin party.

The cause of lead poisoning was not then readily known to physicians aboard the *Erebus* and *Terror*, its visible effects being much the same as starvation and scurvy. In fact, the irony of Franklin's disastrous expedition is that it was probably its very state-of-the-art preparations that caused its downfall. Those huge quantities of food brought by Franklin as part of the ration supply had been concealed in airtight tins lined with lead solder – the very best that industry could offer at the time, but ultimately fatal.

# MAGICAL MYSTERY TOUR

## ENGLAND, 1854

There is a plaque outside Newlyn's Mission to Deep Sea Fishermen depicting a small lugger and recalling a colourful local adventure at the time of the Gold Rush, involving a feat of seamanship unparalleled at the time.

It was a voyage made by seven fishermen from Penzance, Cornwall, to Melbourne, Australia, in a 16-ton fishing boat called the *Mystery,* during 1854–5 – a journey made in an ordinary fishing boat having, of course, neither radio nor any of the sophisticated navigational aids available today.

Following Charles Kelynack's departure to Australia to try his luck in the goldfields, the crew of the family-owned *Mystery* were keen to join him and originally had plans to sell the boat in order to raise the passage money. The combined circumstances of Richard Nicholls, captain of a Welsh trader, coming home on leave and meeting up with his mates and having more than a few pints of ale in a Penzance inn somehow led to the idea of their sailing to Australia in their own boat, with Nicholls acting as skipper.

They made various adaptations to their 36ft (11m) lugger – such as sheathing her bottom with zinc plates and decking her fore and aft – and took on a supply of fresh water and provisions, including salted meat and hard tack. On 18 November 1854 the men – Richard Nicholls, Job Kelynack, Richard Badcock, William Badcock, Lewis Lewis, Charles Boase and P.C. Mathews – set sail, with only a compass, sextant and barometer for navigation, cheered off by enthusiastic crowds on the shore and in escorting boats.

It was four months before their families and friends heard of their safe arrival in Cape Town, where they became the centre of much interest.

Mathews wrote a tantalisingly brief account of their odyssey in 1874:

We were eight days from England to Madeira, and on the 35th day out we made the Island of Trinidad. On the morning of the 17th of January 1855, we arrived at the Cape of Good Hope, being 59 days out. On January 24th, at 6p.m., we got underway from Cape Town and proceeded on our voyage with H.M. mails on board. Nothing interfered with our progress until February 18th [when] we encountered a very heavy gale, which necessitated our riding to a raft for nine or ten hours. Riding to a raft is a system adopted for safety. Ships heave-to under such circumstances.

On February 23rd, another heavy gale visited us ... We again rode to a raft for four or five hours. On the 5th March we met with another very heavy gale ... which compelled us to ride to a raft for 12 to 14 hours. The weather was pretty favourable after that date until we got to our destination.

They were warmly welcomed on their arrival in Melbourne on 14 March 1855, where a Captain Price, son of Sir Rose Price of Trengwainton near Newlyn, offered them hospitality. Most of them eventually returned to Newlyn, eschewing the opportunity to strike it rich in the goldfields. It is ironic, however, that Nicholls, the captain, after making many other voyages, and on the point of starting from London on another, was knocked down by a dray horse and killed.

# TRAGEDY ON ICE
## PRINCE EDWARD ISLAND, CANADA, 1855

In 1829, mail was taken across the Northumberland Strait between Prince Edward Island, New Brunswick and Cape Traverse via fragile ice boats whenever the Strait was frozen over.

The boats were small (about 5½ yards (5m) long and 2 yards (1.8m) wide) and made as light as possible while maintaining their strength. They were equipped with a runner on each side of the hull to allow them to be dragged across the ice floes and snow. Straps attached to the boats and to the crew allowed them to haul the boat, and acted as a safety harness should they break through the ice.

Passengers had to pay $2 for the privilege of going with the crew but still had to assist in getting the boat along – but by paying a double fare they could stay on board during the whole crossing.

However, though it was a distance of only 8½ or 9 miles (13.7 or 14.5km), many accidents happened, one of the better known being taken here from Duncan Campbell's *History of Prince Edward Island* (1875):

When there is a strip of water everyone gets in the boat and it is rowed, and when they came to a field of ice it is hauled up and dragged along. 'Lolly' – that is, a considerable body of snow in the water not frozen, or fine ground up ice – is what is by far the most dreaded, as in it neither can the boat be rowed nor can men walk.

In the month of March 1855 a distressing occurrence took place. The ice-boat from Cape Tormentine to the island, with Mr. James Henry Haszard, Mr. Johnson, son of Dr. Johnson, medical students, and an old gentleman – Mr. Joseph Weir, of Bangor – as passengers, had proceeded safely to within half a mile [0.8km] of the island shore, when a severe snow-storm was encountered. The boat, utterly unable to make headway, was put about, drawn on the ice, and turned up to protect the men from the cold and fury of the storm.

Thus they were drifted helplessly in the strait during Friday night, Saturday, and Saturday night. On Sunday morning they began to drag the boat towards the mainland, and, exhausted – not having tasted food for three days – they were about ceasing all further efforts, when they resolved to kill a spaniel which Mr. Weir had with him, and the poor fellows drank the blood and ate the raw flesh of the animal.

They now felt a little revived, and lightened the boat by throwing out trunks and baggage. Mr. Haszard was put into the boat, being unable to walk; and thus they moved towards the shore, from which they were four or five miles [6.4–8km] distant. On Monday evening Mr. Haszard died from exhaustion.

They toiled on, however, and on Tuesday morning reached the shore, near Wallace, Nova Scotia, but, unfortunately, at a point two miles [3.2km] from the nearest dwelling. Two of the boatmen succeeded in reaching a house, and all the survivors, though much frostbitten, recovered under the kind and judicious treatment which they received.

Mr. Weir lost all his fingers and his two feet, but he did not long survive his loss.

In 1917, the first ferry service began and for the next 80 years, until a bridge was built, islanders travelled to and from the mainland by car ferry.

# NOT JUST A PRETTY FACE

## SAN FRANCISCO, USA, 1857

Mary Brown, the 16-year-old daughter of an English-born family, married Joshua A. Patten, a young clipper ship captain from Rockland, Maine, on 1 April 1853.

Shortly after their marriage, her 26-year-old husband was given command of one of the fastest clipper ships afloat, *Neptune's Car*, and took Mary along on his first trip, which began at the port of New York on a hot July day in 1856. Trouble brewed early on the voyage. The first mate proved so unruly that he had to be put in irons for disregarding orders, demoralising the crew and using every opportunity to delay the ship.

Captain Patten, having discharged his first officer, took over the man's duties himself, not delegating them to another officer. As a result, when *Neptune's Car* swept round the southernmost tip of South America, Captain Patten was up day and night guiding his ship through the treacherous waters off Cape Horn. But, before the ship pulled away from the terrible storms there, Captain Patten, completely exhausted, staggered to his cabin, telling his wife Mary that his head ached abominably and that he felt feverish.

He began to suffer alternating spells of blindness and deafness with periods of complete insensibility. He was clearly dangerously ill.

Mary told the first mate that she had decided to take command of the ship during her husband's illness. His answer was a challenge to the crew not to take orders from a woman, but she called them together and announced that she could plot the proper course and navigate the vessel safely into San Francisco. The seamen agreed unanimously to support her attempt to do something no woman had ever done before: sail a spar-heavy clipper ship out of the treacherous, storm-tossed waters off Cape Horn.

Mary Patten now took observations, worked up the reckoning by chronometer time, laid the ship's courses and performed most of the other duties of the captain of the ship. Meanwhile, snow squalls and violent winds buffeted the ship. The gales became a deafening roar, blowing hills of icy water before them. In this awful struggle to outwit the elements, Mary was so busy plotting the course of the ship and caring for her husband that for 50 nights she did not undress, nor did she get very much sleep.

By the time the ship had come nearly up to the latitude of Valparaiso, Captain Patten had partially recovered from his fever and allowed the first mate to resume limited duties. But, when it was discovered that he was steering the ship out of course and making for Valparaiso, Patten gave orders that under no circumstances was his ship to be taken into any port but San Francisco. Soon after, he had a relapse and for 25 days before the vessel reached port he was totally blind again. All during this time Mrs Patten had yet another burden: she discovered she was pregnant and expecting her first child the following March.

In one fine spurt, however, the clipper logged over 300 miles (483km) in one day but, with San Francisco less than a week's run away, she ran out of winds – a cruel piece of luck. Mary Patten endured this agony with desperate patience. For ten days the clipper lagged off San Francisco, her sails limp under the merciless heat of the sun. When finally a light breeze enabled her to make port, Mrs Patten noted in her log that the trip had taken 136 days.

The Pattens managed to travel to New York and stayed in

a hotel for two weeks before proceeding to Boston, their home. Both in New York and in Boston, however, Mary was besieged by reporters. Her exploits were lauded in the press and leaders of the feminist movement in Boston made the most of her heroism. She was urged not only to join the movement but to make personal appearances on behalf of women's rights.

On 10 March 1857, she went into hospital and gave birth to her son, Joshua Adams Patten. After months of suffering, her husband died in a Somerville, Massachusetts, hospital on 25 July 1857. A fund of $1,400 was raised to tide Mary Patten and her baby over the months following her husband's death.

Sadly, she never fully recovered from the long ordeal at sea. Worn out, she died before her child was four years old, and was buried beside her husband in Woodlawn Cemetery, Everett, Massachusetts.

# THERE'S GOLD IN THAT THAR SHIP, LOOK YOU!

## IRISH SEA, 1859

On 26 August 1859, the 2,719-ton *Royal Charter* steamed out of Hobson's Bay, Victoria, bound for Liverpool. She was a state-of-the-art vessel built specifically for the route to Australia. Built of steel with the lines of a clipper, she possessed auxiliary steam engines to prevent her from being stilled by lack of wind in the tropics.

Almost at the end of her long voyage, and carrying 452 passengers and crew, she sailed into the worst storm that had occurred in the Irish Sea for a century.

After battling across the Irish Sea, the captain called for the Liverpool pilot while off Point Lynas, but the sea was too ferocious for the pilot to go aboard. The captain was faced with a hard choice: he could make his own way to Liverpool without help, or shelter from the severe weather in Moelfre Bay, northwest Wales.

He chose to find shelter, but the *Royal Charter* was demasted and both anchor chains broke under the strain. She was then driven stern first onto the rocks 50 yards (45.7m) from the shore where she broke into two sections. Almost every person on board was thrown into the sea except for 32, who perished as they were hurled against the rocks.

Bodies from the wreck were soon being brought up the hill from the village of Moelfre to St Gallgo's Church, which became the mortuary.

A terrible but not particularly unusual tragedy, perhaps. However, it was soon being claimed that the Welsh villagers had not helped as they should – in fact, they had been more interested in looking for gold!

Many of the passengers were men returning from the Australian goldfields and it was said that some had attempted to leave the ship and swim to shore with their pockets filled with gold dust. About £370,000 worth of gold was estimated to have been scattered in the waves. It was said that Moelfre became rich overnight with many of the large houses built there (and to be seen to this day) having been funded by gold either washed ashore or, according to folklore, looted from the wreck.

Charles Dickens, then at the height of his fame as a novelist and journalist, decided to go to Anglesey to assess the true position. He later wrote an account of his trip in his *Uncommercial Traveller*, in the course of which he revealed the tireless work of a local rector, the Reverend Stephen Roose Hughes.

Hughes had carefully recorded the physical details of each body, its clothing, the contents of the pockets and any detail that might enable an identification of the body to be made. As streams of distraught relatives descended on the village they were greeted by Hughes and comforted by his family. Dickens recorded that Hughes wrote some 1,075 letters in reply to those enquiring after loved ones. In fact, the strain of the event led to his early death in February 1862, and he now lies buried among those who were recovered from the sea. His gravestone bears the following inscription:

His noble and disinterested exertions on the memorable occasion of the terrible Wreck of the 'Royal Charter' are well known throughout the World.

And, in fact, villagers had managed to save a number of people despite the dangerous conditions, with heavy seas sweeping in over flat rocks and dragging many potential survivors to their deaths.

At daybreak, about 5.30a.m., the wreck was seen from the shore but villagers could at first do nothing but stand and watch the tempestuous sea and the helpless wreck.

Their excitement and horror intensified when they saw a man let himself down from the decks by a rope into the midst of the breakers. This was Joseph Rogers, a Maltese able seaman, who volunteered to swim with a hawser to shore and who, though three times driven back by the floods, persevered and succeeded in making the rope fast to the rock – now the only means that remained of landing those on board the *Royal Charter*.

Through the heroic efforts of Rogers and the men of Moelfre, who formed a human chain into the raging seas, 18 passengers, five riggers working their passage, and 18 crew (though no officers) were saved.

Indeed, the community at Moelfre has a long history in lifeboat rescue and over the course of 142 years has saved more than 600 lives.

And, 100 years to the day after the loss of the *Royal Charter*, in October 1959, the coaster *Hindlea*, with a crew of eight, was driven onto Moelfre rocks in a gale with recorded winds of more than 100mph (161km/h). Everyone was rescued.

# THE RUNAWAY SCHOONER

## CANADA, 1866

One day in late 1866, a schooner was securely tied to Lord's Wharf in the harbour at Charlottetown, Northumberland Strait, Canada. She was old and weathered, and without a name plate. The schooner's owners began the scrapping process by removing much of her rigging and running gear.

That evening a severe storm buffeted the boats moored in the harbour. Afterwards, when the schooner's crew returned to finish the job of stripping her down, there was no ship! Only a worn-through rope.

The schooner had run before the wind, out of the harbour and away. Had she realised the crew were ready to dismantle her?

The next day was clear and sunny. Captain John MacLean and a young companion, John Finlayson, suddenly spied a little schooner as they stood on the shore of Hillsborough Bay. The vessel was heading towards Blockhouse Point. They thought it strange to see a vessel without canvas and no obvious crew, so the two men set out in a small boat to investigate and, if need be, salvage the ship. They caught up with the unnamed schooner, and managed to board her, only to lose their own boat.

They expected to find another boat aboard. They didn't realise that the schooner was a runaway with no possessions.

Captain MacLean changed course away from the shoals of the shore and towards deep water. Only then, when

MacLean and Finlayson searched the vessel, did they realise she had been stripped. They found nothing of any great use, only a small remnant of canvas.

The small sail was set and the two men worked unsuccessfully to bring the vessel back to harbour. Then an early snowstorm endangered their lives. The schooner was thrown around and driven far out in the Northumberland Strait. Cold, wet and hungry, the men could only attempt to keep the vessel head on to the waves. Somehow they managed to manoeuvre her into Brule Bay, Nova Scotia, and she was secured in the mudflats.

The people of Brule helped recover the little ship and refit her. The plan was for MacLean and Finlayson to sail her back to Charlottetown and claim the salvage.

On the eve of their departure, the customary party was held. Everyone toasted the success of the coming voyage. The guests were oblivious of the rising winds and developing storm.

The next day, however, as MacLean and Finlayson approached the wharf, a shock awaited them – the schooner was gone again!

Despite furled sails and no crew, the schooner had found her way out of the narrow channel, around Amit Island and along Northumberland Strait to the harbour at Charlottetown. The schooner was back at the wharf she had 'escaped' from the previous week.

When MacLean and Finlayson saw her again, they asked each other the inevitable questions: Was she really unmanned? Was there a phantom crew aboard?

# THE EMPRESS AND THE
# *GAZELLE*

## ENGLISH CHANNEL, 1870

In 1870, following the defeat of France by Germany at Sedan, the Republicans seized their opportunity of overthrowing the emperor. The Third French Republic was proclaimed and, as a frenzied rabble outside the gates of the Tuileries hurled insults at the imperial family, the Empress Eugenie quickly realised that if she did not get away she might well be murdered. Haunted by the fate of the unfortunate Queen Marie-Antoinette, with whom she had felt a deep bond, she knew she must escape from the palace and find a refuge in the city.

Owing to the rapid advance of the German army, the empress was alone and lacking support, except for two foreign ambassadors, her attendant, Madame le Breton, and the famous Monsieur de Lesseps. There was only one hope of escape: by way of the Louvre, with which there was continuous communication.

When eventually Eugenie escaped from the palace, she turned instinctively to her American dentist, Dr Evans, whose mansion, Bella Rosa, lay on the Avenue de l'Imperatrice.

The next day, the dentist took the empress surreptitiously by carriage and train on a trip that lasted two days, buying the silence of innkeepers and avoiding police and soldiers along the way. They finally arrived in the coastal city of Deauville, where Mrs Evans was spending her vacation and where Evans felt he could persuade an English lord, the owner of a small yacht, to take the empress to England. Some members of the palace staff, anticipating the worst, had obtained several travel documents, including a British passport.

Leaving Eugenie at his wife's hotel, Evans sought out Sir John Burgoyne, a member of the prestigious Yacht Club, now the Royal Yacht Squadron, and asked if he would take them across the channel to England in his yacht, the *Gazelle*. Burgoyne at first refused, then, at Evans's urging, put the question to his wife, who shamed him into agreeing. The next day they set out on their voyage across the channel. The dentist later wrote a breathless account of the trip:

The water was very rough, and the tide running full and strong. We cast off, however, and headed for Ryde, whither we had predetermined to go. The night was dark; we couldn't see far ahead; and the winds blew with considerable violence. The sea was too much for our frail craft. All reckoning was lost by some mistake of Sir John's, and everyone on board, except the deck hands, was fearfully sick.

Farther out on the channel the boat was spun round like a mere feather; it seemed impracticable to keep up any sail in such a sea. The men reefed and reefed, but it didn't seem to do any good, for we were shipping buckets-full of water every minute.

Sir John Burgoyne became uncontrollably wild, and declared the yacht would inevitably swamp and they all be drowned. The Empress said calmly that she was prepared, and I buttoned my coat up for the last swim. Sir John managed to spread out his charts on the cabin table, to find, if possible, whereabouts we were, when the vessel gave a one-sided lurch, and away went charts and compasses. 'For God's sake,' he called out to the pilot, 'tell us where we are.' He was altogether *hors de lui,* as the French say, and cursed us for bringing him out to his death.

Seeing his incapacity, I took command of the boat myself, and ordered the pilot to tack, tack, tack. Hour after hour we sailed on thus, in momentary expectation of wrecking. But after a long, long struggle, the sea abated, lights appeared ahead, and pretty soon we were alongside the wharf at Ryde.

They anchored in Ryde Roads and checked into a hotel, whereupon Evans discovered from a newspaper that the Prince Imperial was in Hastings, a short distance away.

He then engineered a reunion between mother and son, during which, as his rather ripe prose suggests, 'The tears of joy flowed abundantly, and her lips murmured words of thanks to Heaven …'

# THE HAUNTED
# (LIGHT) HOUSE
## LAKE MICHIGAN, USA, 1871 & 1885

In 1871, a Captain James Davenport was employed for a wage of $400 to man the lightship at Waugoshance Shoal at the mouth of the Chicago River. In the nineteenth century, before electricity and automation, candles and a complex prismatic structure for magnifying and projecting light (called a Fresnel lens) were used at night during clear weather to warn ships of danger, while handbells were employed when the weather was foggy.

Just seven months after being hired, Davenport found himself caught up in the drama of the Great Chicago Fire. That devastating conflagration that destroyed the downtown area of the city and claimed 300 lives was accompanied by less-publicised and even more deadly blazes the same night in upstate Wisconsin and Michigan, during which two thousand people died and four million acres of farm and prairie lands burned. This catastrophe is now thought to have been the result of a comet fragment crashing into the earth's atmosphere. Eyewitness reports of spontaneous ignitions, lack of smoke and 'fire balloons' falling from the sky bolster this theory.

Whatever the cause, the smoke from the fires, blown in by severe winds, caused a dense fog over Lake Michigan. Which is where Captain Davenport comes in, for there are two apocryphal stories of what he did during the fire and no one, to this day, is sure which is true or exactly *what* happened.

The first story says that Davenport sat in a rocking chair for three days and three nights ringing the bell to warn ships of the nearby deadly reef. To keep himself awake during all this, he placed various pots and pans on his lap so that, every time he dozed off, the pots and pans would clatter to the ground, waking him.

The other story is that, while the dense fog covered Lake Michigan, a schooner – despite the captain's bell-ringing – ran aground on the Waugoshance Reef and the crew swam ashore. For three long and tiresome weeks, they were forced to eat beans as Captain Davenport played his violin with the sounds of Lake Michigan for background.

It remains true, however, that, thanks to the noble efforts of the captain, only seven ships ran aground during the whole ordeal. To this day no one is sure whether it was the violin or the pots and pans or the bell that saved the ships. However, it's said that, on a foggy night, if you listen closely, you might just hear the faint music of a lone violin mixed in with the sound of the waves or the faint sound of pots, pans and a lone bell to the backdrop of the lapping of the waves on the sides of the lightship.

After Captain Davenport retired in 1885, another lightship keeper called John Herman was hired. It's suggested that he enlivened his lonely job by heavy drinking and that, one fateful night, while in a drunken stupor, he locked his assistant in the lantern room as a practical joke. He then proceeded to fall into Lake Michigan and was never seen again.

His ghost was supposed to wander the lightship and caused many of those consigned to keep watch over the shoal into prematurely resigning from the post. Some were said to have had their chairs kicked out from underneath them should they have fallen asleep, and there was even one report of coal found shovelled into the boiler with no one around. If the ghosts still haunt the lightship, they now have it all to themselves. The light was made obsolete and was deactivated in 1910, and two years later it was abandoned. However, despite being used as target practice during the Second World War, it still stands, defiantly on watch.

Today, it is considered one of the most endangered lighthouses in the world. The Waugoshance Lighthouse Preservation Society was formed in 2000 and has undertaken preservation and restoration. It is soliciting funds to rebuild the light, and is seeking an extended lease from the US Coast Guard so that restoration can continue.

# THE *MARY CELESTE*

## PORTUGUESE COAST, 1872

The half-brig *Amazon* was christened in 1861 at Spencer Island, Nova Scotia, and, just 48 hours after taking command of the ship, her captain suddenly died. On her maiden voyage, she struck a fishing weir (a fence), leaving a gash in her hull. While being repaired, the ship suffered a fire, which broke out on board. Not long after, during her third Atlantic crossing, the *Amazon* collided with another ship. Finally, in 1867, the ill-fated ship was wrecked off the coast of Newfoundland and abandoned for salvagers.

But the ship had one last date with destiny. She was raised and restored by an American company who sailed her south for sale. Eventually, in 1872, she turned up at a New York salvage auction, where she was purchased for $3,000 by Captain Benjamin S. Briggs, who raised her sails and headed out to sea towards the Mediterranean with his family – but now the ship was renamed the *Mary Celeste*.

On 3 December 1872, the crew of the *Dei Gratia*, sailing from New York to Gibraltar, found the *Mary Celeste* floating unmanned about 600 miles (966km) west of Portugal. The ship was in perfect condition. The sails were set, her cargo of 1,700 barrels of commercial alcohol were untouched (except for one barrel, which had been opened), a breakfast meal looked as though it had been abandoned in the middle of being eaten, and all of the crew's belongings remained on board. Yet Captain

Briggs, his wife, his daughter and the ship's crew of seven were gone.

Some versions of the story say that the ship's lifeboat was missing, while others say it was still in place on deck. All that seemed to be missing was the ship's chronometer, the sextant and the cargo documents. There was no sign of a struggle, violence, storm or any other kind of disturbance. The last entry in the ship's log was made on 24 November, and gave no indication of any trouble. If this ship had been abandoned soon after this entry, the *Mary Celeste* would have been adrift for a week and a half.

But this was impossible, according to the crew of the *Dei Gratia*, considering the ship's position and the way her sails had been set. Someone – or something – must have worked the ship for at least several days after the final log entry. The fate of the crew of the *Mary Celeste* remains a mystery.

In 1884 Arthur Conan Doyle, writing under a pseudonym, published a story entitled 'F. Habakuk Jephson's Statement' about a derelict ship, which he called *Marie Celeste*. He was paid almost the equivalent of a year's rent for it and it recounted some of the actual events of the *Mary Celeste* with enough added fictional and provocative detail to capture the public interest. In the story, the ship was taken over by a black passenger. He and his fellow conspirators then sailed it to Africa and murdered the passengers and crew. The tale was so vivid that it raised protests from people who mistook the work of fiction for an article.

Doyle was naturally pleased that his short story could be mistaken for a true account of events. He was also delighted those hundreds of readers who understood the work was fictional thought the anonymous author was none other than Robert Louis Stevenson!

After her eerie abandonment, the ship sailed under different owners for 12 years, until her last captain loaded her with a cargo of cheap rubber boots and cat food before deliberately sinking her, and then filing an exorbitant insurance claim for an exotic cargo that never existed. Unfortunately for the captain, his plan fell apart after he'd run the ship onto Rochelais Reef in Haiti: she hung up on the coral and refused to sink. Insurance inspectors investigated and found the worthless cargo. The captain and his first mate were later convicted on charges of what was then known as barratry, which, in the world of shipping, is any unlawful practice committed by a ship's master or crew.

# THE FOSDYK SAGA AND OTHER THEORIES

## ATLANTIC OCEAN, 1872

The *Mary Celeste*, found adrift on 3 December 1872, by the *Dei Gratia*, a bark sailing from New York to Gibraltar (see '*The Mary Celeste*', page 73), is considered by many to be one of the most intriguing and enduring mysteries in the annals of maritime history.

The explanation that seemed most reasonable at the time was the official one put out by the British and American authorities. This suggested that the crew had got at the alcohol, murdered the captain and his family and then somehow escaped to another vessel. But the story does not really stand up. There were no visible signs of a struggle on board, and, if the crew had escaped, some of them would surely have turned up later.

Some accounts say that the he yawl boat – a small four-oared boat carried over the main hatch – was missing, suggesting that at least some of the missing people could have left the *Mary Celeste* in it.

Dozens of theories have been put forward since, ranging from monsters attacking from the deep and aliens kidnapping, to nature's wrath, piracy and mutiny. But no one has ever found any conclusive proof to confirm them. The only 'hard' evidence as to what might have happened are the so-called Fosdyk papers.

According to an article in the *Strand* magazine of London, written by a schoolmaster named Howard Linford and published in 1913 (41 years after the *Mary Celeste* was found), a well-educated and much-travelled employee of his named Abel Fosdyk had left some papers and notes after his death explaining not only the fate of the crew but also the curious cut marks that were found in the bows of the *Mary Celeste*.

Fosdyk claimed that he had been a secret passenger on the ship's last voyage and the only survivor of the tragedy that overtook it. Being a close friend of the captain, Benjamin S. Briggs, Fosdyk persuaded him to give him secret passage because, for some undisclosed reason, he had to leave America in a hurry. During the voyage Briggs had the ship's carpenter build a special deck in the bow for his small daughter. It was the supporting struts for this deck that were slotted into the cuts in the bow planks.

One day, after a lengthy argument with the mate about how well a man could swim with his clothes on, Briggs leaped into the water and started swimming around the ship to prove his point. A couple of men followed while the rest of the crew watched from the deck. Suddenly, one of the sailors swimming around the bow gave a yell of agony. Everyone, including the captain's wife and child, crowded onto the newly built deck, which promptly collapsed under their combined weight. They all fell into the sea, where all were devoured by the sharks that had attacked the first seaman.

Being the only survivor of the shark attacks because of his luck in falling on top of the shattered decking, Fosdyk clung to it as the *Mary Celeste* drifted away. He floated for days until he was washed up half dead on the northwest coast of Africa.

The Fosdyk papers tell a neat tale. But they offer no solution to the mystery of how the ship got to where it was found. And they are wrong on details that should not have escaped an educated man. Fosdyk says the *Mary Celeste* weighed 600 tons. The ship weighed a third of that. Fosdyk also says that the crewmen were English, when they were mostly Dutch. And, most of all, it seems highly improbable that anyone would go swimming around a ship that, according to the *Dei Gratia* evidence, must have been making several knots at the time.

Bizarre as it is, no better explanation than Fosdyk's has so far emerged. And, after more than 140 years, it is unlikely to do so. The enigma of the ship that sailed itself seems destined to puzzle us for ever

Further theories suggest that, in order to take a break from bad weather, the captain of the *Mary Celeste* gave the order to sail to the lee side of Santa Maria Island, where the cook started a fire in the large galley stove to make hot food while other members of the crew furled most of the sails, leaving just enough canvas up to hold her course as they made their way slowly along the lee shore.

Other crew members set about pumping the bilge and doing other chores. When the food was ready, the men aboard stopped what they were doing and ate. After they'd taken a smoke break, the captain gave orders to get under way and the crew went back to work. Some went back to pumping the bilge; others started to set the sails they had just furled. Just then the seafloor started dancing up and down in a violent seaquake – a fairly common phenomenon in the Azores.

During any rapid vertical shifting of the hard bottom, the seabed becomes like a giant transducer, pushing and pulling the water, sending powerful alternating pressure waves towards the surface. The results aboard the ship were as if there were no sea at all under the ship, as though the vessel were sitting on dry land. The deck on the *Mary Celeste* shook violently. The severe vibrations loosened the stays around nine barrels, dumping almost 500 gallons of raw alcohol into the bilge. Fumes spread rapidly throughout the ship. The seaquake also shook the galley stove so violently that it was lifted up from its chocks and set down out of place. Choking on the strong fumes from the leaking barrels, while at the same time seeing sparks and embers flying about from the fire in the cooking stove, the crew panicked and quickly launched the small yawl to try to get away from the pending explosion. However, their worst fears were unfounded because the alcohol did not explode.

Rather, the crew had forgotten, in the panic of the moment, to secure a line from the lifeboat to the mother ship, so the *Mary Celeste,* now crewless, sailed slowly on with only the jib and two other small sails set. As she pulled away from the crew in the small sailing yawl, the men had to decide quickly whether to try to catch up with their ship, or go for the safety of Santa Maria Island, less than 10 miles (16.1km) away. They likely argued about the merits of each course of action, but, knowing they would be disgraced for having abandoned their seaworthy ship and her valuable cargo, they chose to try to catch the *Mary Celeste* in the small yawl, hoping (1) they could overcome her, or (2) the wind would shift and cause her to tack back towards them. Each day of their journey carried them further and further away from the safety of land. They never caught up to their mother ship. Five months later, five highly decomposed bodies were found tied to two rafts off the coast of Spain. One was flying an American flag.

Thus was the fate of the crew of the greatest sea mystery ever told.

# 'DROWNING IN THE DRINK'

## ENGLAND, 1872

While shipwrecks traditionally produce feats of courage and sacrifice, they are also the occasion for some of the baser human instincts to surface. The tale of the *Royal Adelaide*, an iron sailing vessel, is a case in point.

On the night of 24 November 1872, having left London Docks after spending the best part of two months loading a variety of general cargo – including a large quantity of spirits such as rum, brandy, and gin – she was seen passing the Portland Lighthouse off the Isle of Wight a little too close off her starboard bow for comfort. The strong southwesterly wind had quickly strengthened to gale force of such severity, that the ship's captain had decided to turn back to seek shelter from the worst of the weather, but the heavy, blinding rain squalls had blown the vessel fatally off course.

During the afternoon of 25 November, it became clear that the vessel was being driven closer and closer to the western end of Chesil Beach – a long barrier of flint and stone that had posed a threat to sailors for centuries – and, although the coastguards lit blue lights to warn the captain of the dangers of that stretch of coast, the *Royal Adelaide* was now at the whim of the storm and completely unmanageable. To the watchers on the shore it appeared only a matter of time before the vessel struck the beach.

A rescue operation began with a rocket being fired with a rope attached into the rigging of the stricken vessel and a rescue 'cradle' was set in motion. One by one, passengers were hauled to safety. As night fell, however, it became a dramatic scene, the beach illuminated by tar barrels and blue lights while hundreds of spectators now looked on. Shipwreck news spread fast in those days and eager folk arrived in force via the trains of the Weymouth and Portland Railway.

As the ship finally began to break up, the rescue line was lost and the last few survivors on board were swept away and drowned. Nevertheless, all but six of the mainly emigrant passengers and crew had been saved.

By then, it's estimated that more than 3,000 people had gathered to watch the *Adelaide*'s last rites and if the rescue had entertained the watching crowd, the cargo thrown up by the stricken ship was to excite them even more: hats and gloves and boots, herrings, hams, tea, coffee and figs, even livestock as one pig survived by managing to swim ashore. Wholesale looting swiftly began. Many people risked drowning in their efforts to grab items of cargo before either hiding them in the shingle or carrying them away.

But it was when the casks and bottles of brandy and gin were washed up that a near-tragic scene was transformed into one of outright debauchery. The spirits were quickly pillaged by the crowds and, quite soon, many had drunk themselves helpless. Scores of people then fell asleep, drunk, on the cold Chesil pebbles. Friends and neighbours were too busy gathering up cargo to take much notice but, by the following morning, four locals, one a boy of 15, were found dead, killed by a combination of drunkenness and exposure.

Newspapers of the time were loud in their condemnation of such outrageous behaviour, many claiming that the terrible and frightening happenings demonstrated human nature at its worst, the looters' conduct being 'not far removed from the beasts of the field'.

It was later claimed that the eventual death toll among the pillagers reached 20, dwarfing that of the *Royal Adelaide*, whose destruction they had originally come to watch!

# GONE WITH THE WIND!
## ISLE OF WIGHT, ENGLAND, 1878

The tragic sinking of HMS *Eurydice*, a sail-training vessel with hundreds of young naval recruits aboard, off the southeast of the Isle of Wight was a terrible naval disaster that left a deep and lasting impression on the British public.

The *Eurydice* was a wooden, fully rigged, fast sailing ship, originally built in 1843. On the afternoon of 24 March 1878 she was returning from a training cruise in the West Indies with 300 young seamen on board and was sighted by the Bonchurch Coastguard, sailing hard for Spithead.

Twenty minutes later, a heavy squall accompanied by a blinding snowstorm came in suddenly from the land, catching the vessel completely unawares. In less than ten minutes, the squall had passed and the wind had died down, but all that could be seen of the *Eurydice* were the upper sails and rigging above the water a couple of miles off the island. The squall had completely and suddenly turned the vessel around, causing water to rush in through open ports.

A small schooner, the *Emma*, managed to pick up four survivors, but two later died and, although many of the crew were strong swimmers, the waters were little above freezing with snow falling heavily, so most of the survivors simply froze to death before the blizzard ended. The final death toll was 364 officers and men. It was a final recognition that the days of the traditional man-of-war were over.

The tragedy was apparently seen by the young Winston

Churchill, who was visiting the Isle of Wight with his nurse. They watched from a cliff top as the ship capsized.

Not surprisingly, perhaps, given the shock to the national psyche that the event caused, 'sightings' of the ship have continued through the years. On the very afternoon, the Bishop of Ripon was dining with a friend in Windsor when one of the guests suddenly and inexplicably exclaimed, 'Good heavens! Why don't they close the portholes and reef the sails?' Asked to explain himself, he replied that he didn't know, but had had a vision of a ship coming up the Channel under full sail with her gun ports open while a great black squall attacked her.

Several people since have witnessed sightings of a phantom, three-masted ship that vanishes if approached. Many of these have been blamed on freak reflections of light on mist, yet in the 1930s a submarine was forced to take evasive action to avoid striking a full-rigged ship, which promptly vanished in just the spot where the *Eurydice* sank.

And in May 1998 Prince Edward (the Earl of Wessex) claimed to have spotted the phantom galleon while filming for a TV series on the Isle of Wight. He was telling the story of the *Eurydice* when someone suddenly exclaimed that there was a three-masted schooner out at sea. They waited until it drew closer to the shoreline, but it then vanished.

The film crew claimed to have captured the ghost ship on video but, in another strange twist, the tape jammed in the machine when they went to view it. Sailing-ship enthusiasts added to the mystery by saying they knew of no vessel in the area at the time Edward saw the ghost ship.

HMS *Eurydice*'s bell now hangs in St Paul's Church, Shanklin; Gerard Manley Hopkins composed a poem:

Too proud, too proud, what a press she bore!
Royal, and all her royals wore.
Sharp with her, shorten sail!
Too late; lost; gone with the gale.

# GHOSTLY GALLIONS REACH

## ENGLAND, 1878

The paddle steamer *Princess Alice* was launched at Greenock, Scotland, in 1865. Originally known as the Bute, she served on the Thames excursion routes for 120 years and became one of the most popular passenger steamers on the Thames at that time.

On 3 September 1878, the *Princess Alice* made the routine trip from Swan Pier near London Bridge to Gravesend and Sheerness, carrying hundreds of Londoners, many of whom had been visiting Rosherville Gardens in Gravesend. A day trip down the Thames to Gravesend, Sheerness and Margate was a traditional family outing for generations of Londoners.

That evening, she returned from Sheerness with about 700 passengers, many of whom were listening to the band as the steamer approached North Woolwich Pier. She passed Tripcock Point and turned into Gallions Reach. At precisely this time, the *Bywell Castle* was steaming towards her.

The *Bywell Castle* was a far larger vessel. She was a steam collier of 890 tons. She had just been repainted at Millwall Dry Dock, and was returning to Newcastle to pick up a cargo of coal destined for Alexandria in Egypt. To Captain Harrison on the bridge of the *Bywell Castle*, the *Princess Alice* appeared to be coming across his bow, making for the north side of the river. He therefore altered course accordingly, intending to pass safely astern of her. But the passenger steamer suddenly changed course directly into the path of the oncoming collier. The bows of the collier struck the steamer just forward of the starboard paddle box, almost cutting her in two.

Before long, the vessels in the area were picking up bodies rather than survivors. Nearly 500 were recovered in the first week after the collision. Many of those who died had not been thrown into the water. When the two halves of the *Princess Alice* were raised from the Thames scores of bodies were discovered piled around the exits.

As news of the disaster spread, crowds gathered at North Woolwich Pier and at the London Steam-Boat Company's offices in the City. Company spokesmen read out the names of the survivors to those who waited anxiously for word of family and friends.

Few were to hear good news. Though some were identified from their clothes, despite considerable efforts, around 120 bodies were buried as unidentified, for in Victorian times few people carried any form of identification and many bodies, having been in the water for some considerable time, were unrecognisable.

While the local coroner was presiding over the inquest (the jury would return a verdict of death by misadventure), the Board of Trade was conducting its own hearing. It concluded that both commanders had shown poor judgement and recommended that two vessels under steam should always 'pass each other on the port side'.

The *Princess Alice* Memorial in Woolwich cemetery was erected consisting of an ornamental marble Irish cross, with an inscription saying:

It was computed that seven hundred men, women, and children were on board. Of these about five hundred and fifty were drowned. One hundred and twenty were buried near this place.

On another face of the pedestal it is stated that the memorial was erected 'by a national sixpenny subscription, to which more than twenty-three thousand persons contributed'.

Woolwich Council itself spent £1,380 in recovering and burying the dead, as the county justices, who had always previously paid such expenses, repudiated the charge. The Treasury voted £100 towards the bill, and the ratepayers paid the rest.

Gallions Reach became known as 'Haunted Reach' after the disaster, and the *Bywell Castle* was to disappear without trace in the Bay of Biscay just four years later while returning from the Mediterranean. She is still listed officially as 'missing'.

On 20 August 1989 on the Thames in London, a lightly built pleasure boat – the *Marchioness* – sank when she was cut through by another, much larger iron-built ship, the dredger *Bowbelle*. Of 131 people on board the *Marchioness*, 51 were drowned.

Despite the recommendations of the *Princess Alice* inquest jury in 1878, history had repeated itself.

# THE MYSTERIOUS LOSS OF THE *ATALANTA*

## BERMUDA, 1879

HMS *Atalanta* reached Bermuda on 29 January 1879. That much is known. Then she left Bermuda two days later – probably turned away because of yellow fever cases aboard – and turned into an Atlantic mystery.

HMS *Atalanta* was a training ship. She had been launched at Pembroke Dock in West Wales in 1844 as HMS *Juno*, and used in the Pacific until she became a virtual hulk. The Portsmouth Dockyard police had the ship as their headquarters until they found permanent accommodation on the site of the original commissioner's house.

After the loss of the *Eurydice* (see 'Gone with the Wind!', page 82), *Juno* was towed back to Pembroke Dock and refitted with suitable accommodation for ordinary seamen under instruction. She was renamed – against the superstition of many seamen – and commissioned as HMS *Atalanta* at Devonport on 17 September 1878. Her officers, under Captain Francis Stirling, had a high reputation and there was no immediate concern when the *Atalanta* left Bermuda and became overdue.

Then, at the end of April, when hopes were receding, a massive search was launched.

The British gunboat *Avon* found wreckage from an unidentified vessel off Azores, near the route customarily used by training vessels. In April 1880 there was a claim that the steamer *Tamar* had sighted a capsized copper-bottomed ship. The captain later denied the report.

On 20 April 1880, the British ship *Wye* left Gibraltar and searched near Vigo Bay, Spain, where portions of a wrecked vessel had been washed ashore. Nothing new was found.

Eight days later, a message in a bottle was found from the *Atalanta*. It proved to be a hoax.

On 2 June 1880 a captain arriving at Queenstown from Demerara said he had passed a makeshift raft containing two corpses dressed in white uniform. Another vessel later made the same sighting.

Thirteen days later came another bottle with another message: 'April 17, 1880: training ship *Atalanta*. We are sinking in longitude 27 degrees, latitude 32 degrees. Any person finding this note will please advertise in the daily paper. John L. Hutchings, Distress.'

On 21 June 1880 a piece of barrel stave was found on the beach at Cow Bay, Nova Scotia. It contained a message written in lead pencil: 'ATALANTA going down, April 12, 1880; send this to Mrs. Mary White, Piers, Sussex. James White.'

A committee of inquiry was set up, but only to investigate the seaworthiness of the ship. No witnesses were called and no explanation for *Atalanta*'s disappearance was ever found. The *Atalanta* was simply lost to the Atlantic.

The public quickly linked this loss with that of the *Eurydice*, especially as both ships had had recent refits. In December 1880, *The Times* disclosed that nine ships of Her Majesty's navy had sunk without trace since 1840.

All that remained of the *Atalanta* was speculation.

Another victim of the Bermuda Triangle? Sabotaged by American terrorists? Or just a jinxed ship?

# THE FISHERMAN WHO LOST HIS FINGERS
## NEWFOUNDLAND, CANADA, 1883

In January 1883, Howard Blackburn, a young Nova Scotian fisherman, signed on with the Gloucester schooner *Grace L. Fears*. The *Grace L. Fears*, captained by Alec Griffin, was bound for the Burgeo Bank, a rich fishing ground 60 miles (96.6km) south of Newfoundland, in search of halibut.

At daybreak on 26 January, Howard Blackburn and his mate, Thomas Welsh, set out in a small boat, a dory, in search of halibut. They rowed their rugged 18ft (5.5m) boat – with flared end and a flat bottom – away from the *Grace L Fears* and began to set their trawl.

Later that day, with a storm brewing, the captain ordered the dorymen to retrieve their trawls early but, as the men worked to haul in the trawl, the weather worsened. The other crews were already rowing back to the schooner just as Blackburn and Welch finished hauling the end of their trawl. As they began pulling for the schooner, the squall hit. Snow swirled around, reducing visibility. More ominously, because of a wind shift, they were leeward of the schooner and forced to row against the wind and mounting seas. They rowed and rowed, and periodically sounded their horn, but it was drowned out by the howling wind.

By nightfall, they still had not reached the schooner. Later, when the snow stopped, they were able to glimpse its lights in the distance but its position indicated that they were no closer to it. They anchored and spent a frigid night, continuously doused by the icy spray. At dawn, the *Grace L. Fears* was not in sight. Blackburn and Welch were alone in their dory as the gale blew.

The men decided to row for the Newfoundland coast, which was 60 miles (96.6km) or more to the north. The seas were treacherous and they were in peril of capsizing. Rowing against the gale was useless and they were forced to heave to. The men took turns bailing and rowing to keep the dory head to wind.

While bailing the dory, Blackburn lost his mittens in the wash. He was so preoccupied with trying to keep the boat afloat, that it wasn't until Welch pointed out that his hands looked funny that Blackburn finally took notice. Realising that his hands were freezing and would soon be useless, Blackburn slowly forced them to grip the oars. Within a short time they had become frozen claws.

The gruelling ordeal continued. It was a constant struggle to keep the dory upright. The men had to pound the ice encrusting the dory to prevent it from building up and sinking the boat. Blackburn's frozen hands were battered in the process. The wind was unrelenting and the frigid air engulfed them.

Nightfall came on the second day but brought no salvation. During the second night, Welch began to falter and Blackburn had to carry on the struggle by himself. As daylight came on the third morning, Blackburn realised that his dorymate had frozen to death.

Blackburn continued to row all through the third day with his dead dorymate in the stern. His thirst tormented him. He rowed and rested, his lonely labour continuing. Night came, and the cold was unrelenting. On the fourth day, the seas were calm and he rowed on. By now his hands were worn to the bone. Each pull of the oars brought agony. By late afternoon he could see the white outline of the coast. Another day passed and, finally, on the fifth night after being separated from the schooner, Blackburn reached the fishing settlement of Little River on the Newfoundland coast.

Although he had survived, Blackburn was forced to undergo a painful recovery from his frostbite. He eventually lost all the fingers on both hands and half of each thumb. He also lost several toes, two from his left foot and three from his right.

Blackburn's remarkable story of survival spread fast and he soon became a legend. After his recovery, Blackburn drifted down from Newfoundland and settled in Gloucester, Massachusetts, an old fishing port that fitted his temperament. The people of Gloucester raised funds which enabled Blackburn to become the proprietor of his own saloon.

# THE 'CUSTOM OF THE SEA'

## ATLANTIC OCEAN, 1884

A wealthy Australian barrister purchased a yacht, the *Mignonette*, in Essex. Although the boat was not the sturdiest, the owner decided to have a crew sail it to Sydney for him rather than send it as deck cargo. He hired Thomas Dudley as captain, and Dudley recruited Edwin Stephens as mate, Edmund Brooks as able seaman and a 17-year-old boy, Richard Parker, as ordinary seaman. They left in late May 1884 and experienced several weeks of smooth sailing. Later the weather turned foul, and Dudley decided to turn off the main trade route. The winds, however, dogged them. Then suddenly, in the late afternoon of 5 July, a heavy wave smashed against the stern of the boat and sprang loose its timbers.

The *Mignonette* sank in less than five minutes. The four seamen just barely managed to get into their lifeboat, a 13ft (4m) open dinghy. Unfortunately, the emergency supply of water that they had hastily thrown overboard next to the dinghy was swept away by the waves. Only Dudley had brought anything with him into the dinghy: two tins of turnips and a sextant.

Sixteen hundred miles (2,575km) away from the closest shore, their only hope was to get on the main trade route and be picked up by another ship. However parsimoniously rationed, the two tins of turnips were quickly consumed. Occasional rainfall permitted the men to collect some unsalted water in their oilskins. Parker, much sicker than the others, quickly ate his rations; the rest were able to hold out longer. On the fourth day they spotted a turtle asleep on the water, hauled it on board and fed on it for nearly a week, even eating the bones and chewing on its leathery skin. They tried to catch some fish, but with no success. Their lips and tongues parched and blackened from thirst, they took to drinking their urine. Eventually Parker and Stephens resorted to drinking seawater, then thought to be certain poison.

On the nineteenth day, feeling more dead than alive, Dudley proposed that one of them, to be chosen by lots, be killed for the rest to feed on. Using a lottery to select the one who was to die was a practice common in the late nineteenth century known euphemistically as the 'custom of the sea'.

Brooks would not hear of it and Stephens was hesitant, and so the idea was temporarily abandoned. Dudley next tried to persuade Stephens. He no longer talked about drawing lots. Parker evidently was the sickest, and he had no wife or children. It seemed only fair, Dudley reasoned, that he be the one killed. Finally, Stephens agreed. Dudley walked over to where Parker lay at the bottom of the boat, his face buried in his arms. 'Richard,' he said in a trembling voice, 'your hour has come.' 'What? Me, sir?' mumbled the half-conscious boy, uncomprehendingly. 'Yes, my boy,' Dudley repeated and then plunged his penknife into Parker's neck.

For the next four days all three, including Brooks, who had objected to the killing, fed on the boy's body, even drinking his blood. On the twenty-fourth day of their odyssey they were sighted by a German boat, the *Montezuma*, heading home from South America. Of the three men, only Brooks was able to clamber aboard; the rest had to be carried. Parker's remains, still in the dinghy, left no doubt about what had happened and both Dudley and Stephens completed the tale as soon as they had recovered sufficiently. The

German crew, however, continued to treat them with the utmost kindness.

On 6 September 1884, the *Montezuma* sailed into Falmouth. The survivors were taken to the Customs House and closely questioned. It did not occur to them that they had done anything criminal. Dudley told of their adventure with something resembling gusto and even insisted on keeping the penknife with which he had killed Richard Parker as a memento. They were stunned when they were put under arrest and charged with murder. The upright Dudley immediately insisted that he was the ringleader and that Brooks was completely innocent. Brooks was indeed discharged and became the prosecution's chief witness.

Throughout the trial and the preparations preceding it, public sympathy was almost entirely on the side of the 'cannibals'. When Dudley travelled from Falmouth to London to meet his wife at Paddington Station, people took their hats off as he passed. The trial judge described Dudley as a man of 'exemplary courage'. The mayor of Falmouth was threatened with murder for having arranged the men's arrest. The prosecutor was similarly threatened, if he obtained a conviction. And, most remarkably, Daniel Parker, Richard Parker's eldest brother, forgave Dudley in open court, and even shook hands with him

The jury on the case was not permitted to render a verdict, for fear it would simply acquit the defendants, but was merely allowed to determine the facts. Nor did the trial judge render a judgement. Instead, by way of a highly unorthodox procedure, the case was brought before a five-judge tribunal, presided over by Lord Chief Justice Lord Coleridge, who, in his summing up, expressed doubt as to whether a situation of necessity had truly existed, refused to recognise self-preservation as an all-justifying end and declared that a rule permitting the killing of someone in situations of necessity would be virtually unworkable. The defendants were found guilty as charged and sentenced to death.

For all its rhetoric, the court, however, did not want to be taken too seriously. A pardon by the Home Secretary had been arranged in advance, and, when it came time to pronounce the death sentence, the judges did not even wear their black hoods as is customary on such occasions.

The defendants were released from prison six months later. Brooks had already gone back to sea, but neither Dudley nor Stephens was enamoured of the idea. Stephens settled down near Southampton and apparently supported himself through odd jobs. He continued to be absorbed by the events on the dinghy and over time went quietly mad. Thomas Dudley emigrated to Sydney, Australia, where he became a small shopkeeper and managed to keep his past history a secret. He, too, was haunted by memories of the dinghy, which, according to one report, he tried to relieve by great quantities of opium. He died as the first victim of the bubonic plague that hit Australia in 1900.

# WHAT SHALL WE DO WITH THE HEADLESS SAILOR?

## SAN FRANCISCO, USA, 1890

The Norwegian ship *Squando* was a vessel blighted long before it set sail. Several men were killed during its construction, which led to one of their widows cursing the ship and everyone who would subsequently sail in it. She then committed suicide in order to make the curse stick – and she succeeded beyond her wildest hopes!

In 1890, the *Squando* docked off the Embarcadero in San Francisco. It was at this point that Captain Nels Erikson discovered his wife had been having a romantic tryst with Lars Gunderson, the first mate of the ship. Whether under duress or because she was ashamed of her faithlessness, Erikson's errant wife then assisted him in the murder of Gunderson. She plied Gunderson with liquor and, when he was sufficiently inebriated, held his arms as her husband chopped her lover's head off with an axe.

There are, it must be said, differing versions of the killing. One has the captain summoning Gunderson to his cabin where he cut his head off with a cutlass in front of his horrified wife. Another has the captain's wife merely being stalked by the first mate rather than becoming involved in a full-blown affair. Whatever the method of murder, or the extent of the betrayal, however, all versions of the story tell of the murderous couple tossing Gunderson's headless corpse into the San Francisco Bay while keeping his head in a bucket in their room, apparently under their bed.

Soon afterwards, the headless torso of the slain first mate was discovered floating in the San Francisco Bay. Captain and wife then fled San Francisco (although once again the story has an alternative version, this one suggesting that the San Francisco police discovered the missing head that the couple had stashed away in their bedroom. The couple were then arrested and subsequently hanged).

Despite the conflicting story lines, what happened next certainly confirmed the potency of the widow's terrible curse. The ship's owners hired a new captain who shortly thereafter was killed during a baffling mutiny of the crew. It was rumoured that the crew had been unnerved by a spectre, perhaps of the murdered first mate. What's more, the next two captains of the *Squando* met with similar sinister fates, both being murdered in their cabins without explanation. There was talk of weird voices echoing through the ship, of baffling incidents involving the ship's equipment malfunctioning. Finally, in 1893, the ship's entire crew, unnerved by the apparent cursed nature of the ship, deserted it in Bathurst, New Brunswick, and efforts by the owners to hire a replacement crew proved fruitless.

Perplexed as to what to do with the ship, the Norwegian consul eventually hired two night-watchmen to guard it and, while discussions over its future were held, to investigate the ghost stories. This simply led to more problems. On the very first night, the hired men quit in a hurry, fleeing the ship in terror. They had encountered, they claimed, a headless apparition roaming the hallway in front of the captain's cabin. There had been a series of disturbances, with ship's tackle – spars, ropes, hand-spikes – littered across the deck. What's more, they had been woken during the night by supernatural visitations, someone tugging at their sleeves, and hollow whispers entreating then to 'Go, go, at once!'

Over the next few weeks, it was the same story – watchmen first hired but then almost immediately quitting in panic. Unable to hire anyone to work on it, the owners were finally forced to demolish the poor, doomed *Squando*. The *Chatham Gazette* of 24 March 1893 reported that the hull and materials of the barque had been auctioned at Bathurst, realising $2,600. There's no mention of the auctioneer including the ship's ghosts in the inventory!

# WHEN *BRITANNIA* RULED
# THE WAVES

## ENGLAND, 1890s

The *Britannia* was commissioned by the Prince of Wales, later Edward VII, from the drawing board of G.L. Watson, acknowledged as one of the finest yacht designers of his time. The yacht was launched from the Partick yard on the Clyde in April 1893. With her long out-curving stem, high rig and great sail area, she was a radical advance on the clipper-bowed low-aspect yachts of the 1880s and early 1890s both in looks and performance, winning her first offshore race in the Thames Estuary from the great yachts *Valkyrie II*, *Calluna* and *Iverna*.

By the close of her first season's racing that year *Britannia* had scored 33 wins from 43 starts. This debut was no fluke, for in her second season she won all seven races for the big-class yachts on the French Riviera (the prince's favourite sailing area), and then returned to trounce the 1893 America's Cup winner *Vigilant* in home waters. By the end of her fifth season, not only had her prize money paid for her upkeep, but it also went a long way towards reimbursing the £10,000 that she had cost to build.

The 1897 season saw a sad decline in big-class racing, and *Britannia*'s own racing flag was hauled down and not seen for another 15 years. During that time she was to change hands six times, twice being repurchased for the Prince of Wales by royal command, once to act as a trial horse for Lipton's America's Cup challenger *Shamrock I*, and finally, after Edward VII's coronation, to be used as the royal cruising yacht. With raised bulwarks and a reduced rig, she was cruised around the coast of Britain by the king and queen to the popular acclaim of the people, but missed the revival of the big racing class in 1906.

After the death of Edward VII, the *Britannia* officially became the property of King George V, formally commodore of the Royal Harwich Yacht Club, and then its patron. Two years later, in 1913, she was back on the racing scene, entered in the handicap classes with albeit limited success by the king's representative, Major Philip Hunloke, whose later association with the yacht was to become legendary. During the years of the First World War, the *Britannia* languished unattended in a mud berth, until the king brought her out for racing in 1920.

Her return to the regatta circuit was spectacular. Still with her outdated rig, she met the challenge from the fastest modern big yachts, including the cutters *Nyria* and *White Heather*, and the American-built schooner *Westward*.
George V was so chuffed by *Britannia*'s performance that he ordered a complete refit to put her into competitive racing trim for the 1922 season. This was money well spent, for in 1923 she won 23 flags out of 26 starts – not bad for a 30-year-old yacht! That year also saw the first big-class yacht racing with a Bermudan rig, but, despite altering *Britannia*'s rig in 1926 and 1927, the king did not finally agree to 'go Bermudan' until 1931. His stubborn affection for the gaff rig proved to be a correct sentiment, for the *Britannia* fared badly under her Bermudan sails, despite being handled brilliantly by Sir Philip Hunloke.

By 1934 she was hardly competitive with the new highly technical J-class racers beginning to appear on the scene. Her last race was sailed in 1935 at Cowes.

The following year, 1936, King George V died leaving instructions that, if none of his sons wanted the yacht, the *Britannia* should be broken up. As this was the case, it was left to Sir Philip to make the arrangements for her last departure. With all her spars, gear and refinements stripped away, her bare hull was towed from the Medina at midnight on 9 July 1936, out past the Needles light and St Catherine's Point to a position somewhere to the south of the Isle of Wight. There she was scuttled and sent to rest beneath the waves. The yard foreman had placed a simple garland of flowers on her stem-head.

# GALLEON IN THE MIST

## ISLE OF WIGHT, ENGLAND, 1891

The *Etruscan* was a galleon launched at Woolwich in 1638, which sailed for over 50 troubled years. In 1650 there was a mutiny on board when nine of her crew were hanged. The following year saw her so badly damaged in a storm that she had to be almost re-built. In 1655, a collision with a naval pinnace in the Thames resulted in the death of six men.

Two hundred years later in 1891, the brigantine *Halsey* under the command of Captain Arthur Brake was en route from Lisbon to Gravesend, 10 miles (16.1km) south of the Isle of Wight. Early one morning, one of the watchmen saw that a ship was sailing dangerously close to them. It was a galleon.

Imagine the astonishment of the crew to find themselves borne down upon by a ship, fully rigged with three masts and three tiers of guns and the name 'Etruscan' (seen by some) on her side. Only the prompt action of the helmsman avoided a collision.

As the men watched, the galleon vanished into the mist. Some crewmen said it had been a ghost ship and no good would result. Indeed, soon afterwards a sailor broke his leg falling 30ft (9.1m) to the deck.

On docking at Gravesend, the whole crew testified that they had passed so close to this ship that they had been able to see the other crewmen's terrified faces. They could also hear commands being given by their officers. One man was heard to scream towards the *Halsey*, 'It's the *Black Prince*!'

Some crew members of the *Halsey* were later asked to draw a picture of what they had seen. These drawings could all be identified as being of one of a British man-of-war, either the *Sovereign of the Seas* or the *Etruscan*.

There can be no explanation of these events, witnessed by so many, but at least one twist to the tale remains.

In 1690, in the waters of the Isle of Wight, the *Etruscan* collided with a British frigate and sank with the loss of 130 lives. The name of the frigate with which she collided? The *Black Prince*!

# THE NEW ENGLAND 'TITANIC'

## NEW ENGLAND, USA, 1898

In a few fateful hours, somewhere overnight between 26 and 27 November 1898, decisions were made that led to the worst maritime disaster in the history of New England. The stately *Portland* was a beautiful, luxurious 281ft (85.6m) sidewheel steamer with 42ft (12.8m) beam but, with a draught of only 11ft (3.4m), it was cruelly unsuitable for the heavy seas it met that night.

As the *Portland* prepared to set out to sea, a powerful storm, swirling out of the Gulf of Mexico, headed up the East Coast. It would fatally combine with another storm heading from the Great Lakes, a deadly mix that would ultimately produce hurricane-force winds and wreck or sink 140 vessels and devastate New England coastal communities.

But on India Wharf, as passengers began to arrive for the night steamer, unusually busy following the Thanksgiving holiday, there was no sign of what was to come.

Throughout the day, warnings of the impending storm were passed from the Boston weather bureau to the Boston agent of the Portland Steam Packet Company of Maine, C.F. Williams, but preparations to sail continued unchecked.

Some say that the Portland-based general manager of the line, John Liscomb, was so fanatical about his steamers leaving on time that none dare contradict him, though it is known he tried to get a message to Boston to delay departure by two hours. But he could not get through. Some say the captain, Hollis H. Blanchard, thought he could outrun the storm to Portland. For whatever reason, at 7p.m. the whistle of the *Portland* sounded and she headed out to sea. It was the last confirmed time she was seen.

The course Captain Blanchard normally took carried him across Broad Sound and then up to Salem and Marblehead and on to Cape Ann and Thatcher's Island. From there it was a straight run into Portland. Captain William Thomas of the fishing vessel *Maud S* reported that he thought he saw the *Portland* about 3 miles (4.8km) south of Thatcher's Island. But it was snowing and the visibility was getting worse. By 10p.m. the wind had shifted to northeast and picked up to over 30 knots (55.6km/h) with gusts up to 60 knots (111km/h). Shipping all along the coast raced for shelter. Those that were unable to reach a safe harbour were beached and wrecked along the south and north shore of Massachusetts. Ships in Boston Harbour were driven into the wharves and splintered.

A little after 9a.m., the schooner *Ruth M. Martin*, south of Cape Cod, saw a large white steamer and put up a distress flag to attract attention. The *Martin* escaped but the *Portland* did not.

That evening the storm began to abate. Two surfmen walking along the beach spotted a life belt and, dashing through the breakers, retrieved it. It was stencilled with the words 'Steamer Portland of Portland'. The next morning along the south shore of Cape Cod between Race Point and Peaked Hill, wreckage of the side-wheeler came ashore along with bodies. There were no survivors.

The *Portland* disaster, known to some as the New England *Titanic*, saw more than 200 people die but the blame for the tragedy has remained a matter of debate. Why did Captain Blanchard ignore storm warnings? Was he so enamoured of his own sailing skills that he thought he could conquer the blizzard? When did the *Portland* sink?

Watches found on the bodies of victims were practically all stopped at 9.15 – but was that p.m. or a.m.? And where did she finally sink?

Like so much else about the SS *Portland*'s end, the answers have remained a mystery. Until 30 August 2002, that is, when specialists with the National Oceanic and Atmospheric Administration confirmed that the steamship's location had been found at an undisclosed spot in the Stellwagen Bank National Marine Sanctuary, and showed the first pictures of the wreck.

In 2008, five Massachusetts scuba divers became the first to reach the steamship and made three successful dives where they found the wreck strewn with artefacts such as stacks of dishes, mugs, wash basins and toilets, but no human remains. However, because of the depth of the wreck site, some of their dive lights imploded and they could only explore the site for a short while before needing to return to the surface.

# 'THAT INTREPID HERO'
## ATLANTIC OCEAN, 1899

After he had survived gales and cold in a dory and lost all his fingers (see 'The Fisherman Who Lost His Fingers', page 92), Howard Blackburn's saloon in Gloucester, Massachusetts, eventually became one of the best-known saloons on the North Atlantic seaboard.

According to Joseph E. Garland in his *Lone Voyager*:

> There he stood behind the bar, cigar clenched in the thumb stub of one hand ... After he had filled one of the big pot-bellied beer glasses from the tap, he squeezed the stem between the creases in both hands, set it on the bar and gave it a flourishing shove down the length. Blackburn's was a workingmen's club; fighting, frivolity and loud talk were not allowed.

But Blackburn's days of adventure at sea were not over. He designed his own boat, the *Great Western* – sloop-rigged, 30ft (9.1m) in length and 8ft 2in (2.49m) in beam – and set sail from Gloucester harbour at 2p.m. on 18 June 1899 to cross the Atlantic. His goal – Gloucester, England. Contemporary American press reports suggest that some ten thousand people were on hand to bid him a safe voyage as he cast off from the Seven Seas Wharf and steered through the busy inner harbour, heading into the Atlantic.

The *Great Western* was provisioned with enough food and

water for 90 days – but for five men. Asked before he left why he was carrying so much, Blackburn replied, 'I might meet someone on the road who needs provisions, so I'm taking an extra supply.' The sloop was designed with safety in mind rather than for speed. Blackburn had extra large reef points put on the main sail to enable his fingerless hands to cope.

Soon after leaving the Massachusetts coast, Blackburn was attacked by rheumatism. And, with his right foot and leg swelling badly, he was comparatively helpless for eight days – able only to hoist the riding sail and jib. Recovering quickly, he found that on 26 June he was fit enough to raise more sail in a bid to make up for lost time. He had travelled just 250 miles (402km) in those first eight days. The first part of the voyage saw Blackburn heading northeast for some 800 miles (1,287km) until he turned east for the Atlantic crossing when he was off Newfoundland.

With a vast experience of these waters, he slept during the afternoons and attended to the vessel at night because of the fog that he knew so well. But, after passing Newfoundland, he returned to sleeping, where possible, at night. There was, however, little time to sleep as he battled against rain and westerly winds. According to his log, he was making some 6–14 miles (9.6–22.5km) a day. At times, he was at the wheel for more than 36 hours without sleep. But after passing the 40th meridian, he met better weather and the wind was more favourable. He was able to sail from 4a.m. to 8p.m., and sleep at night.

The good weather allowed Blackburn to make good speed, and his log records his estimate of making Lundy Island in the Bristol Channel 'in 48 to 50 days'. It was not to be. When he was about 1,000 miles (1,609km) west of Ireland, the *Great Western* was becalmed for two days before an easterly wind came up.

According to the English *Gloucestershire Chronicle*, the public had considerable doubts as to whether or not

Blackburn was really making an attempt to cross the Atlantic in a small boat, 'and unassisted'. But the doubts were laid to rest at 4.15p.m. on Friday, 18 August, when the *Great Western* arrived at Kingroad, a part of the Severn estuary off Portishead, north Somerset, where a large crowd of people had congregated in the dockyard. There was also an official welcoming committee of local dignitaries on hand to greet the sailor, who had already been hailed locally as 'that intrepid hero'.

The following Tuesday, he was the guest of the Theatre Royal in Westgate Street, Gloucester. The manager, Mr Burge, had reserved a box bedecked with the Stars and Stripes and the Union Flag. Before the entertainment began, Blackburn was introduced as 'the wonder of ocean navigators' before being cheered loudly. He sat through the play *The Queen of the Camellias* and at the end of the performance the pit orchestra played 'Yankee Doodle' before the British national anthem.

Blackburn would accomplish another solo Atlantic crossing aboard his sloop the *Great Republic*. He also journeyed by schooner to the Klondike in search of gold.

He died in 1932 aged 73 while asleep in his apartments above his saloon in Main Street, Gloucester, Massachusetts.

# THE PHANTOM BOAT

## EIRE, 1900

It was in 1900 that Jamsie Quain saw the phantom boat. One day he was tending his land in Dysert, Ardmore, in the Irish county of Waterford. At the end of the long field was a well, the overflow from which was used to feed the cattle runs down to the cliff. There he had a potato garden at the cliff edge near the stile.

It was wintertime and early in the New Year. The previous night had been very stormy, and, although the day was dry at sea, it was dangerously rough. As he was digging, he glanced up and saw an object out on the deep. As it approached, he realised it was a ship's lifeboat. There were about a dozen men in it rowing and another steering. He saw them change seats a few times. Assuming there had been a wreck, he went over to the station to call the coastguard and they both went back to the cliff. The boat was drawing near and almost below them. But the cliffs were too steep to descend. The crew looked cold, wet and hungry.

The two observers called out and Jamsie Quain waved to them with his cap. The sailors took no notice but kept rowing in closer until they came around the headland into the calm water in the bay. Suddenly, to the amazement of the onlookers, they turned out to sea again. This was unbelievable, since the men looked overcome with fatigue. Yet they were heading out from the sheltered waters and the safety of dry land, back into the danger of the open sea.

Quain and the officer hurried down to the pier, and quickly got a crew together that included Pat Troy and Maurice Flynn. They got the sail up, set off in pursuit and soon began to catch up with the boat. The wind was from the south and they lost the shelter of the land as they headed towards Mine Head. The officer persuaded the men to go on a bit further until they got within about 200 yards (183m) of the lifeboat.

After that, they could get no nearer, although they tried everything possible. They shouted, but the sailors gave no sign of hearing them. The wind was rising and gradually the lifeboat started to pull away from them.

Maurice Flynn suddenly said, 'Turn back, Quain, or we'll all be lost. You're following dead men.' Quain reluctantly did so. They were only just in off the corner of the head when a sea broke on top of Seán Spán, a sunken rock off Ardmore Head where a Spanish ship had once been wrecked. A wave big enough to drown a liner sometimes headed across the bay and, if it caught them, they would all be lost. They turned back to Ardmore.

The coastguard officer phoned Mine Head Lighthouse and alerted the rescue services along the coast. Enquiries up and down the coast were in vain; the sailors were not picked up and the boat was never seen again.

At cow time that evening in Dysert, the officer met Jamsie Quain and asked, 'What did you think of that business today?' Quain said he didn't know. The officer continued. 'If you were in that boat all night or maybe a few nights and suffering wet, cold and hunger, would you jump ashore and take your chances with the natives if you saw them waving to you as you approached or would you turn out to sea again?'

Quain said he'd go ashore. Finally the officer asked, 'Quain, have you ever heard of a phantom boat?' He hadn't but after further discussion they concluded it must have been such a vessel. Some days later they heard that a large vessel had been lost out at sea about a week previously, with no survivors.

# A 'MOST BRUTAL THING'
## NEW YORK, 1904

When Adele Wotherspoon died on 26 January 2004, she was 100 years old. As a six-month-old baby, then called Alice Liebenow, she had survived the *General Slocum* steamboat disaster, in which an estimated 1,021 people died. The youngest *General Slocum* survivor had lived to become the oldest.

On 15 June 1904, about 1,300 people set off for the seventeenth annual Sunday school picnic of St Mark's Evangelical Lutheran Church. The church, based in a Germanic area of New York City, had spent $350 on chartering the *General Slocum*, a 264ft (80.5m) long paddle-wheel excursion steamer reminiscent of the great Mississippi steamboats. All but a hundred guests were women and children.

Adele Liebenow was the youngest of a family group that included her parents, her two sisters, three aunts, an uncle and two cousins. On a sunny Wednesday morning they looked forward to their journey to the Locust Grove Picnic Ground at Eaton's Neck on Long Island. As the boat left the East River pier at Third Street at 9.40a.m., the church band on board played, 'A Mighty Fortress is Our God'.

Forty minutes later, joy turned to horror – a fire started in a forward storage room and the steamboat quickly turned into an inferno.

'Children whom the flames had caught on the forward

decks rushed, blazing like torches, to their mothers,' said the periodical *Munsey's Magazine*.

The captain refused to steam for shore and instead proceeded at top speed through the perilous waters of Hell Gate towards North Brother Island, 1 mile (1.6km) ahead. His inexperienced crew were unschooled in fire drills, and the emergency equipment was virtually useless. Lifeboats were stuck to the deck with paint, the life jackets had decayed to dust and fire hoses disintegrated under water pressure.

When the *General Slocum* reached North Brother Island, it was without the upper deck, which had collapsed. Fire boats steamed into the disaster area to douse the flames, but the paddle steamer's hurricane deck disintegrated into burning timber and the *General Slocum* eventually burned down to the waterline. The victims either died in the flames or drowned after being knocked into the water.

The river men did their best to help the victims, but a yacht following the burning steamboat simply put about and steamed away. Flying the pennant of the New York Yacht Club, the yacht made no attempt to pick up any of the nearby women or children in the water.

The estimated death toll of 1,021 included Adele's sisters, Anna, aged three, and Helen, who was six. Adele was in the arms of her mother, also named Anna, when the fire started. Her mother covered her face, and, with her clothing on fire, jumped into the river.

Adele's father, Paul Liebenow, helped his badly burned wife and daughter ashore and then searched for his missing daughters. The body of Helen was never found, but Anna was eventually identified.

Adele Martha Liebenow's 100-year life was shaped by the *General Slocum* disaster. A year later, at the Lutheran Cemetery in Queens, she unveiled a monument – sculptures of four figures symbolising despair, grief, courage and belief in the hereafter – commemorating the 61 unidentified dead. As her mother held her up so she could pull the cord, Adele dropped her doll.

The Lower East Side of New York City became haunted with memories of black crêpe on door after door and two hundred hearses rolling slowly across the Williamsburg Bridge.

Paul Liebenow, co-owner of a Manhattan restaurant, remained on a nervous edge until his death in 1910, six years after the fire. He had kept the tiny brown leather shoes his daughter Anna had worn on her last day and the white cotton dress Adele had worn when unveiling the monument. Adele eventually became a teacher in New Jersey. She retired in 1961.

The ship's captain, William Van Schaick, who had ironically once sold fire extinguishers, was eventually convicted for negligence and sentenced to ten years in prison. He served three years in Sing Sing before being released on parole in 1911 and pardoned a year later.

The burned-out hulk of the *General Slocum* was later raised and sold for $1,800. Converted into a barge and renamed *Maryland*, she sank laden with coke off Atlantic City.

The *General Slocum* disaster is referred to by James Joyce in his celebrated novel *Ulysses*. A character refers to the *General Slocum* disaster as being the day before Joyce's strange and legendary 'Bloomsday', thereby setting the novel in actual time. 'Terrible affair that *General Slocum* explosion,' the character says. 'Terrible, terrible! A thousand casualties. And heart-rending scenes. Men trampling down women and children. Most brutal thing.'

# A SAD BUT AMAZING COINCIDENCE

## ENGLISH CHANNEL, 1908

On 11 June 1908, a little fishing boat named *Fear Not* manned by her owner, 60-year-old William Rowe and his 17-year-old son, set out from Plymouth to the Eddystone whiting grounds. At about four o'clock in the afternoon the boat returned to Sutton Harbour in the Cattewater, the stretch of water where the mouth of the River Plym merges with Plymouth Sound.

Observers later testified that Rowe himself was sitting upright in the thwart of the boat with his arms folded, gazing out beyond the bows. His son, meanwhile, leaned upon the tiller steering the boat. The wind was light and as the *Fear Not* came along slowly, the fishermen on the pier-head hailed to the two men to know what sort of catch they had aboard. They received no answer as neither of the figures in the boat stirred in the least. This attracted some curiosity and as the boat came alongside another little fishing smack, a startling discovery was made. Rowe himself was dead and his son appeared quite unconscious of his surroundings, like a man in a trance.

Later, the boy was able to explain the mystery to some extent. He said that, at the end of their fishing stint, his father hove up the anchor and then dropped back into the sitting posture in which he was found and never spoke nor stirred again. Failure of the heart's action brought about by heavy exertion in the excessive heat was suggested as the likely cause of death. When the son realised that his father had expired he said he felt like one in a dream and he could only remember blankly steering the boat for Plymouth.

Amazingly, just a fortnight later, another fishing boat named *Fear Not* hailing out of Brixham Harbour – no more than 30-odd miles (48.3km) from Plymouth – also met with tragedy. Close by Bishop's Rock, in St George's Channel in the Irish Sea, the British steamer *Irak* was heading for Liverpool when it encountered dense fog. As a consequence, neither master nor mate nor the lookout in the crow's nest caught more than a passing glimpse of the small vessel with brown sails heading to the westward, her sails drawing to a light breeze from the northeast, and apparently under good control.

It was the *Fear Not* – and before anyone could react, the *Irak* had cut her completely in two from port to starboard. No sound or cry made by anyone on board the *Fear Not* was heard on the *Irak*, and no lifebuoys were thrown overboard at the time of the collision. However, immediately it was realised what had happened, the helm was moved, the engine-room telegraphs reversed, and every effort was made to save life. A boat was got away smartly, and the ship remained in the vicinity of the accident until 3p.m. but all five of the crew of the *Fear Not* perished.

# SHIP WRECKED BY A METEOR

## PACIFIC OCEAN, 1908

London, 12 March. As reported in the *Marlborough Express* of Queenstown, New Zealand, on 29 April 1908, a sailing ship named *Eclipse* was on its way from Newcastle to San Francisco when it encountered a storm and three lives were lost.

A tale of shipwreck more vivid by far than the strangest imaginations of the writers of romance and adventure reached Queenstown last night. The sailing ship *Eclipse*, 1,469 tons, was on a voyage from Newcastle to San Francisco. She had been at sea for 85 days when she was overtaken by a terrible hurricane. Lightning, followed by deafening peals of thunder, lit up the sky. Suddenly a meteor struck her fore top-mast, which fell in splinters to the deck. The meteor crashed right through the deck, and, tearing a large hole in the hull, fell into the sea. Water immediately poured into the ship. The pumps were set going, and for four days and nights the crew worked to save their ship, snatching sleep in short spells as they could. No effort could keep the ship afloat, however. Captain Lessen and his crew of 15 were compelled to take to the boats, and a few hours later they saw the ship founder. The men spent 15 days in the open boats under a scorching sun. Two biscuits and two gills of water formed each man's allowance for the day. They shaped a course as best they could for the Sandwich Islands, 900 miles (1,448km) from the spot where they were wrecked.

Their sufferings reached a climax on the thirteenth day, when three men died. Their bodies when thrown overboard were instantly devoured by the sharks which followed the boats. Some days later they sighted a small island, and on the following day the boats reached its shore. The helpless sailors were carried on the backs of the natives to places of shelter. Their sufferings were then at an end, and they were conveyed later to Honolulu.

# JOSHUA SLOCUM (ALMOST) MEETS CHRISTOPHER COLUMBUS

## ATLANTIC OCEAN, 1909

Born on 20 February 1844, in Annapolis County, Nova Scotia, by the Bay of Fundy, Joshua Slocum ran away at the age of 14 to work on a fishing schooner, but soon returned home. In 1860, however, he left for good when his mother died and shipped as an ordinary seaman on deep-water sailing ships and merchant vessels to Europe and the US.

He obtained his first command on the California coast in 1869, and sailed for 13 years out of San Francisco to China, Australia, the Spice Islands and Japan.

On 24 April 1895, at the age of 51, in the rebuilt 37ft (11.3m) sloop *Spray*, Slocum departed from Boston Harbour, Massachusetts, on his famous single-handed circumnavigation of the globe. He returned, sailing into Newport, Rhode Island, on 27 June 1898 after sailing around the world, a passage of 46,000 miles (74,028km).

At one point during that three-year voyage he became sick. As he lay in his cabin a storm hit but he was too ill to go topside and shorten the sails. He says he lost consciousness for some hours but, after he awakened, the storm was still raging. As he looked out of the companionway, he was amazed to see a tall man at the helm, looking for all the world like a foreign sailor. The large red cap he wore was cockbilled over his left ear, and he had shaggy black whiskers. According to Slocum, the sailor took off his hat and assured him that he had come to do him no harm, but was from Columbus's crew on the *Pinta* – one of the three ships Columbus had taken to the New World in 1492 – and had come to help him.

The strange man bade him lie quiet, so that he could guide his ship for him.

When Slocum woke up the next morning, he had recovered enough to go on deck. The gale had calmed a bit and the sun was shining. The man was nowhere to be found. Everything that had not been secured had been washed away. The sails were still set, but under the circumstances should have been very damaged due to the storm. Also, the *Spray* had made 90 miles (145km) that night right on course.

With this little bit of whimsy, Slocum started a tradition that still delights voyagers today. The pilot of the *Pinta* has become the patron saint of all solo circumnavigators.

On 14 November 1909, at the age of 65, Slocum set out on another lone voyage to South America, leaving from Vineyard Haven on Martha's Vineyard, but was never heard from again.

# LOST CHILD OF THE *TITANIC*

## ATLANTIC OCEAN, 1912

The *Titanic* and its terrible demise has been the source of many books, films and even plays since the doomed ocean liner hit an iceberg off the Grand Banks of Newfoundland and disappeared beneath the icy surface of the Atlantic. However, strange echoes still reverberate down the years, proof, if proof was needed, that such catastrophes are always more than simply physical events.

In 2014, over 100 years on from the disaster, perhaps the last mystery involving one of the most tragic of all tales connected to the sinking was resolved. Perhaps …

Loraine Allison was a two-year-old girl travelling on the liner with her family, parents Hudson and Bess Allison, plus seven-month-old brother Trevor. They were rich, her father a Canadian entrepreneur, and were travelling with an extensive entourage of servants. Following the collision, the Allison family could have escaped along with the majority of first- and second-class passengers, but for some reason Hudson, Bess and Loraine remained on board. Some reports state Bess and Loraine were placed in a lifeboat, but that they returned to the ship, either because Bess would not leave her husband, or because she was distraught, not knowing that her son was safe. Trevor, meanwhile, had been snatched up in the confusion by his nurse, Alice Cleaver, and taken to a lifeboat. The two survived the disaster. The three remaining members of the family were last seen huddled together on the boat deck, near the officers' quarters, as others were struggling nearby to free the last of the collapsible lifeboats for use. It was later stated that Loraine Allison was the only child in first and second class to die (53 of 76 children in third class perished). Her body was never found. Only her father's body was recovered.

Almost 30 years later, however, in 1940, there came a sensational twist to this tragic story. A woman called Helen Kramer appeared on a radio show called 'We, the people', and claimed to be Loraine Allison! She said she had been saved at the last moment when her father had placed her in a lifeboat with a Mr Hyde, who then brought her up as his own. According to Kramer, Hyde had lost trace of his own three-year-old daughter in the confusion. After rescuing Loraine, Hyde had raised her as his own child in England where she said she attended boarding school before moving to the US. Kramer claimed Hyde had revealed the truth to her shortly before his death after she requested her birth certificate. As a final twist, Hyde was not his real name. He was, in fact, Thomas Andrews, who had been *Titanic*'s designer and builder and who was thought to have died in the sinking.

Despite these far-fetched claims, Kramer provided enough personal details to convince distant relations of the Allison family that she was telling the truth. However, immediate family members rejected her claims outright and when she died in 1992, it seemed the story died with her.

In 2012, however, during a series of forums dedicated to the *Titanic* on the centenary of its sinking, Kramer's granddaughter, Debrina Woods, claimed she had found documents in a suitcase belonging to her late grandmother substantiating her claims. She then attempted to contact the Allison family. They responded by hiring lawyers to demand she terminate her activities and to stop her scattering her grandmother's ashes over the Allison family plot, in Chesterville, Ontario. It was suggested that, had Woods' claims been substantiated, she would be eligible to inherit much of the family wealth as Trevor Allison had died. Woods denied harassing the family and insisted she had no interest in their money. 'It is rubbish to suggest it is about money or claim I have harassed anyone. This was never about money. My grandmother never wanted money and I don't either.' Nevertheless, Woods had already set up a website selling posters, mugs and mouse-mats highlighting her grandmother's claim and said she planned to write a book about the story.

*Titanic* experts, meanwhile, were divided. While many were sceptical, some were supportive of Woods' case. In fact, the debate led to the establishing of an identification project by Tracy Oost, a forensic scientist at Laurentian University, Canada, and *Titanic* researcher. DNA testing of both the descendants of Kramer, and from the family who had died on the ship, was carried out and revealed no genetic link, exposing the decades-old claim as a hoax. Further investigation suggested Helen Kramer was in fact raised in Michigan, as Evangline Irene Lee Hyde.

David Allison, grandson of Hudson's brother Percy Allison, said, 'The Allisons never accepted Mrs Kramer's claim, but the stress it caused was real. It forced my ancestors to relive painful memories described to me as immeasurable sorrow and unending grief.'

Nancy Bergman, a sister of David's, said, 'These DNA results have uncovered a colossal fraud that has haunted my family for years. It was all about the money …. Debrina wants to write a book and no doubt there are others out there who want to profit from our story. It is our story. Leave us in peace.'

Professor Oost said, 'It is good to have a resolution here, but we mustn't forget that this is all about one of the more tragic of tales to come from the *Titanic*.'

The ruling meant Loraine kept the unhappy claim of being the only child from first or second class to die in the sinking.

# GREAT LAKES DISASTER

## GREAT LAKES, USA, 1913

From 7–12 November 1913 there raged the greatest storm
ever to strike the Great Lakes. It was also the greatest storm
in the history of inland navigation and one of the grimmest
on record. It raged for 16 hours continuously at an average
velocity of 60mph (96.6km/h), with frequent spurts of 70
(113km/h) and over.

Shipmasters testified that they ran through waves at least
35ft (10.7m) high. In the midst of the storm, the wind on
Lake Huron swung from northwest to northeast so that it
frequently blew one way while the sea ran in the opposite
direction. These forces subjected the ships to what the
US Life-saving Service called 'incredible punishment'.
Incredible, indeed – the association later tabulated the
disaster at 248 lives lost and 71 vessels lost or damaged
sufficiently to require official notation.

The *Charles S. Price* and the *Regina*, two modern steel
bulk freighters 400–550ft (122–168m) in length and up to
nearly 8,000 gross tons, were up-bound a few miles from
each other in lower Lake Huron when they were last seen
under steam. The hurricane was so furious, however, that
it turned the *Price* around, so at the moment of the ships'
loss, they were going in opposite directions.

The *Regina* vanished without a trace. The *Charles S. Price*
was turned upside down and was, therefore, unidentifiable
for ten days, floating near Port Huron before she went to

the bottom with her dead. But a mystery surrounds the last hours of both ships.

The body of the chief engineer of the *Price* was washed ashore wrapped in a life preserver from the *Regina*. Other bodies from the *Price* also wore life belts marked 'Regina'. But no *Regina* men were ever found with life belts from the *Price*.

Two men – one from each ship – were washed ashore dead and frozen, their arms about each other. Did the ships collide? The body of the *Price*'s steward, Herbert Jones, was washed ashore with his cook's apron still on as though he had just started or finished preparing a meal. Therefore, it is assumed the disaster happened fast.

The suggestion has been offered that men of the *Regina* saw that the *Price* had turned turtle; that their ship ran to assistance; that the *Regina*'s crew hurled life belts to the aid of the *Price*'s men and then their ship was overcome in her turn. No one knows. No one has ever found out why.

Somehow, in the hurricane and blizzard, the crews must have met and intermingled on their way to a quick death in the freezing water.

# DULCIBELLA AND *THE RIDDLE OF THE SANDS*

## EIRE, 1916

Known as the Yachtsman's Classic, *The Riddle of the Sands* was written by Erskine Childers, a House of Commons clerk, in 1902 and subtitled *A Record of Secret Service*. One of the first great spy novels, *The Riddle of the Sands* is set during the long, suspicious years leading up to the First World War and heralded a long series of espionage books during that period.

As much a sailing book as a thriller, *The Riddle of the Sands* draws on Childers's considerable knowledge of the sea and provides a precise account of sailing practice. The book begins as Carruthers, a wealthy, jaded and vain Foreign Office civil servant, receives a phone call from an old but unglamorous friend (Arthur Davies) inviting him on a sailing holiday around the East Frisian Islands in the Baltic in the yacht *Dulcibella*.

The two uncover a mysterious German military project and jump headlong into adventure as amateur spies. The book was intended as a wake-up call to the British government to watch their North Sea defences.

It is clear from Childers's original logs, however, that *The Riddle of the Sands* is based closely on his 1897 Baltic cruise in *Vixen*, a 30ft (9.1m) converted ship's lifeboat. A decade later, Childers, a skilful sailor, turned fiction into fact. He aligned himself politically with the fight for Irish Home Rule and engaged in gun-running for the Irish Volunteers. On 12

July 1914, as the rest of Europe was poised on the brink of world war, Childers, his wife and a handful of other Home Rule supporters boarded the 50ft (15.2m) ketch *Asgard*, to meet the German tug *Gladiator* on the high seas.

On the return trip to Ireland the grossly overloaded *Asgard* was hit by the worst storm seen in the Irish Sea for 30 years and at one point Childers had to lash himself to the wheel. They also had to sail through the British fleet – which was unexpectedly being inspected by George V off Spithead.

They finally made Howth Harbour on the morning of 26 July and the guns were quickly unloaded by members of the Irish Volunteers. With the cargo delivered, Childers and company sailed back to England and into the First World War, which had begun just a few days after the Howth excursion. The weapons would be later used to arm the Irish Republicans for the Easter Rising of 1916.

Childers subsequently became embroiled in the Irish Civil War and was court-martialled and sentenced to death on 24 November 1922.

The *Asgard* was used for some years as a sail training ship before being placed in the yard of Kilmainham jail in Dublin, now a museum. Later, a heated debate took place in the Dáil (the Irish parliament) as to what should happen to her. Should she be restored to her original condition but kept in the museum, or restored to sailing condition and used as a sailing memorial not only to Childers but also to her builder Colin Archer, a legendary designer at the turn of the last century?

In 2001, the 28-ton yacht was 'released', hoisted by crane over the wall of Kilmainham jail into the hands of a consortium of businessmen determined that the vessel should be restored to its former beauty.

In 2007 restoration work began focusing on preserving as much as possible of the original wooden hull and its metal supports before replacing pieces with new material. Since August 2012 the restored *Asgard* and related artefacts have been on permanent display in Collins Barracks, Dublin, in an exhibition titled 'Asgard: The 1914 Howth Gun Running Vessel Conserved'. Nessa Childers MEP and her brother Prof. Rory Childers were the guests of honour at the official opening.

It was too late for Childers's real *Dulcibella*, however, a smaller yacht once owned by him, which eventually ended her days at the Lymington Slipway in Hampshire. In 1948, following unsuccessful attempts to try to restore her as a lasting memorial to Childers, it was decided to break her up. A piece of the keel was sent to Mrs Molly Childers, Erskine Childers's widow, in America.

# WE'LL MEET AGAIN
## NORTH SEA, 1916

Arnt Berthelsen was born in 1900, the son of a boat builder in Mandel, Norway. He began his seafaring career as a 14-year-old cabin boy out of Oslo. Two years later Berthelsen survived a devastating shipwreck. The most bizarre event, however, came 30 years later, when his past caught up with him in the United States.

In the winter of 1916, the barque *Sagitta* voyaged from Savannah, Georgia, to Kallenburg, Denmark, laden with ordinary cargo. The First World War meant a nervous passage through the heavily mined North Sea. But it wasn't the mines that got them. The *Sagitta*, an unarmed merchant vessel, was attacked by a German submarine.

At the first salvo of the submarine's heavy deck guns, a piece of steel struck Arnt Berthelsen's forehead and he was nearly blinded by the blood. Then, as the *Sagitta*'s captain ordered the topsails backed to heave the ship to, the submarine fired a torpedo. The *Sagitta* started to sink stern first into the icy waters. A lifeboat was launched and 19 sailors took to the oars. The German submarine offered no rescue assistance.

Arnt Berthelsen and his mates were stranded in their lifeboat on a freezing, stormy ocean. They had nothing to eat or drink. They grew wild with hunger. One night some of them killed the ship's dog and ate him raw. Another night they drank snow from their sleeves and the ship's rail.

They spent five long days and nights on the lifeboat. Some of the men cut their own throats. Others threw themselves overboard. The weather was so severe that some died anyway. But Arnt Berthelsen rowed on. The 16-year-old found he had more stamina than most of the older men.

Eventually, the skiff washed up in a small Norwegian fjord. A newspaper boy, out on his delivery route from a nearby village, sounded the alarm. At first, the locals thought that every castaway was dead. Then they discovered four survivors, covered in ice and blood, barely alive.

The Norwegian newspapers ran the story. The readers were shocked that a German submarine could sink an unarmed merchant ship.

Arnt Berthelsen recovered and returned to sea. He served on a variety of ocean-going vessels, and eventually became a captain. Years later he emigrated to Brooklyn, New York City, a popular area for Norwegian emigrants.

Berthelsen commuted daily by subway and met a lot of Norwegians on the journey. One day, as a newsboy passed through the subway car selling newspapers, a Norwegian stranger started a conversation. 'You know,' he said, 'I was a newsboy myself, in my village during the First World War. As a matter of fact, I was once a bit of a celebrity because of it.'

'Oh, is that so?' answered Arnt Berthelsen.

'Yes. You might recall a big news story back then, when the Germans sank one of our sailing merchant ships? The survivors were discovered on the beach by a young newsboy, you remember? Well, I was that boy who found them! What do you think of that?'

Arnt Berthelsen smiled. 'Well, it's good to see you again! You see, I was one of the four survivors you found in the lifeboat that day! What do you think of *that*?'

They enjoyed a grand reunion on a New York subway, 30 years after meeting in an icy North Sea fjord.

# THE HAUNTED SUB

## NORTH SEA, 1916

The U-65 was one of a class of 24 U-boats built to operate from the ports of occupied Belgium during the First World War. But the U-65's two-year lifespan brought only a catalogue of ill luck that eventually haunted all who sailed in her.

The U-boat's keel was laid at the naval dockyard at Wilhelmshaven in June 1916. Construction was in its first few days when the boat claimed her first victim. A heavy metal girder slipped from the crane tackle as it was being lowered into the hull. One German workman was killed instantly and another died in hospital from injuries. Then three men died as a result of poisonous fumes in the engine room.

Five men had been killed before the boat had even put to sea. More tragedy came with the U-65's first sea trials. A seaman, sent forward to inspect hatches, was swept overboard and lost. Worse was to come when the captain gave the order for the U-65's first dive. Instead of levelling out at 30ft (9.1m), as the captain had ordered, the boat sank to the sea bottom following a fracture in a forward ballast tank. By the time that the U-65 rose again, freeing herself from the seabed 12 hours later, floodwater had reached the giant batteries and caused toxic poisoning. Two men died in hospital as a result, and other crew members were badly affected.

In February 1917, the U-65 was commissioned into the Imperial German Navy and placed under the command of Oberleutnant Karl Honig, a very experienced U-boat officer. The U-65's active service complement was three officers and 31 ratings. They soon became aware that the boat was jinxed.

As torpedoes were being loaded in readiness for the U-65's first patrol, a warhead exploded. The second officer and eight seamen were killed, and nine others were seriously wounded.

As the U-boat was being towed back into dry dock for repairs, one hysterical seaman swore that he had seen the ghost of the dead second officer standing on the prow with folded arms. Another seaman, a man called Petersen, claimed to have seen the same ghost. Petersen deserted a day before the U-65 set out on her first patrol.

So far a total of 17 men had been killed in five separate incidents. And the U-65 was yet to face combat!

During the course of her first active patrol, several seamen claimed to have seen the ghost of the second officer. On one occasion the duty officer was found sobbing on the bridge after a vision of the second officer standing on the prow. Three seamen who joined the boat at Zeebrugge described the ghost before they had been warned that the boat was haunted.

In February 1918, a patrol in the Dover Straits brought several more sightings of the ghostly second officer, including one time when he allegedly spoke with a seaman in the forward torpedo room. When the U-65 docked at Bruges, the crew were very grateful to be on dry land again, even though the docks were being attacked by British aircraft. However, when Oberleutnant Honig set off down the boat's gangplank, on his way to the Officer's Club, he was decapitated by shrapnel. His headless body was carried back on board the U-65.

That night nine men, including an officer, saw the ghost

of the second officer standing beside the canvas shroud of the captain's corpse. Every member of the crew requested a transfer from the U-65 and the boat was placed into reserve at Bruges. A German naval padre, Pastor Franz Weber, conducted a service of exorcism.

By June 1918, German Naval Command had suffered heavy U-boat losses, so the U-65 was called up for patrol duties. On 30 June, she set out on what proved to be her last patrol. Early in the morning of 10 July, the US submarine L-2 was patrolling 9 miles (14.5km) off the coast of Cape Clear, Ireland, at periscope depth. The American captain spotted a German U-boat moving slowly on the surface. It was the ill-fated U-65. The American prepared his submarine for attack. He was set to give the order to fire two torpedoes when there was a shattering explosion that ripped the U-65 from stem to stern. That American captain later said that immediately before the explosion he was amazed to see the solitary figure of a German naval officer standing on the prow of the U-boat.

# THE MYSTERY SHIP OF DIAMOND SHOALS

## MAINE, USA, 1920

As with many great mysteries, the last voyage of the *Carroll A. Deering* started with several twists of fate. She was built in Bathe, Maine, in 1919, a huge five-masted schooner designed for cargo service, and in August 1920 she was preparing to set sail from Norfolk, Virginia, with a cargo of coal bound for Rio de Janeiro.

At the last minute, the captain, William M. Merritt, was suddenly taken ill and left the ship. The *Deering* company rushed to get a new captain, Willis B. Wormell, from Lubec, Maine.

On 8 September, the *Deering* was under way. Her voyage went well and she docked at Rio de Janeiro, where the cargo was unloaded. However, it was later reported that Wormell confided in an old friend, a Captain Goodwin, that the first mate, McLellan, was worthless and a trouble maker.

On 2 December 1920, the *Carroll A. Deering* set sail, bound for Portland, Maine.

When the schooner was next sighted, she was off Cape Lookout Lightship, North Carolina. The date was 29 January. The lightship keeper, Captain Thomas Jacobson, was hailed by a crewman on the *Deering* who shouted through a megaphone, 'We've lost both anchors and chains in the gale off Frying Pan Shoals – forward word to our owners!'

The lightship's engineer photographed the schooner, its

sails set, jib topsail slacked down, and seemingly in decent shape, though it was noted that its crew were scattered about the deck in undisciplined fashion.

The schooner then continued on its way and glided out of sight along the coast. Late the next afternoon, a northbound steamship sighted a five-masted schooner 25 miles (40.2km) southwest of Diamond Shoals Lightship and 'steering a peculiar course', apparently aiming straight for Hatteras itself.

On 31 January 1921, a lookout, scanning the ocean with a telescope from a cupola atop the lifeboat station at Hatteras, spied a five-masted schooner, all sails set, aground on Outer Diamond Shoals, not quite 10 miles (16.1km) away. A surfboat, launched through the breakers, was able to get within 500 yards (457m) of the vessel. No signs of life were observed. When four days later the sea finally abated sufficiently to enable a salvage tug out of Norfolk to put a crew aboard, what was found was a deserted ship, with steering gear ruined, wheel broken, binnacle box bashed in, rudder disengaged from its stock and stock driven through the deck, dory and yawl gone, and running lights and red distress lanterns aloft burned out. In the galley were a pot of coffee, a slab of spareribs and some pea soup. The ship's papers, log, chronometer and navigation instruments were missing.

By then the winter ocean, its waves breaking over the deck, had shredded several sails, dug the wooden hull deeply into the sands and twisted the ribs and plankage beyond saving. The Coast Guard cutter *Manning* attempted to tow the *Deering* from her place but, due to the rough waters, had to cut the towline and destroy the ship with mines. Thus, the *Carroll A. Deering* perished on 4 March 1921.

An investigation followed, undertaken by five separate departments of the US government. There was plenty of speculation about what happened. That the crew may have done away with the captain and their comparative lack of seamanship resulted in the wreck. Rumrunners had commandeered the schooner for their purposes and then scuttled the vessel. Bolsheviks had seized the *Carroll A. Deering* and kidnapped its crew to work in the navy of Mother Russia.

These speculations reached a fever pitch when one Christopher Columbus Gray, a 35-year-old navy veteran, produced a message in a bottle he claimed to have discovered while searching the beach in April following the wreck.

The message was reportedly written by the *Carroll A. Deering*'s engineer and said a pirate vessel had control of the ship and was removing the *Deering*'s crew. Handwriting experts authenticated the message, and suddenly there was the possibility that the *Deering*'s crew were still alive. But that hope faded when experts employed by federal investigators ruled the message in a bottle a forgery, and Gray admitted his lies.

For decades, pieces of the *Carroll A. Deering* were scattered across the Outer Banks – on beaches and in private collections. But the sea never gave up its secret about the doomed schooner. Perhaps it was jinxed from the start. After all, it had been launched on a Friday, 4 April 1919, christened with flowers, and had cats on board – the only survivors.

# SAILING'S SERIAL KILLER?

## USA, 1920s

In 1917, convicted murderer Carl Panzram escaped from Oregon penitentiary, calmly walking off while three other escapees were shot down. After taking on a new identity and working as a merchant seaman, he arrived in New York in 1920. After robbing the home of a wealthy ex-politician,

he bought a boat and embarked on a ten-year murder spree.

He registered the boat – the *Akista* – under the alias John O'Leary and sailed it up the East River, through the Long Island Sound and onto the Connecticut coast, breaking into dozens of boats on their moorings along the way, stealing anything he could get his hands on. He eventually moored at the New Haven Yacht Club, where he settled in for a time, enjoying the hot weather, drinking and planning his next killings.

He visited Manhattan's Lower East Side, and noticed scores of visiting sailors on shore leave from their ships docked along the East River. He realised that many of them were looking for work on outgoing freighters or local boats.

'I figured it would be a good plan to hire a few sailors to work for me, get them out to my yacht, get them drunk, commit sodomy on them, rob them and then kill them. This I done.'

For several weeks, he picked out one or two victims and told them that he had work on board his yacht anchored off

City Island at the foot of Carroll Street and needed some deckhands. He remained there for the entire summer of 1920. In 1920, City Island was a secluded, maritime community of fishing boats, sail manufacturers and residents who tended to their own business. At first, most people paid little attention to 'Captain John O'Leary'.

'Every day or two I would go to New York and hang around 25 South Street and size up the sailors,' Panzram said. When he persuaded them to come on board his yacht, they would work for maybe a single day. 'We would wine and dine and when they were drunk enough they would go to bed. When they were asleep I would get my .45 Colt automatic, and blow their brains out!'

He then tied a rock onto each body and carried them into his skiff, rowing east into Long Island Sound near Execution Lighthouse, and waited for the rising tide to take the prisoners. There, not 100 yards (91.4m) from the lighthouse, Panzram dumped his victims into the sea.

'There they are yet, ten of 'em. I worked that racket about three weeks. My boat was full of stolen stuff,' he later wrote. But City Islanders soon grew suspicious of the *Akista* and its skipper. Panzram realised he had to change venue. He sailed down the coast of New Jersey with his last two passengers until he reached Long Beach Island, where he intended to kill them both. In late August 1920, a huge gale hit and the *Akista* smashed to pieces against the rocks. Panzram swam to shore and barely escaped with his life.

The two sailors made it to the beaches just north of Atlantic City and quickly disappeared into the Jersey farmlands, never realising how lucky they had been to escape certain death.

During the early summer of 1923, Panzram made his way back to Providence, Rhode Island, where he stole a yawl out of one of the many marinas around the bay. By then, he was an accomplished sailor who had navigated the seas in dozens of countries in all sorts of weather conditions. The boat was a fine craft, 38ft (11.6m) long and outfitted with all the best equipment.

He set sail for Long Island Sound, an area that he knew well and where he felt comfortable. He docked at New Haven for weeks at a time and would go out at night, cruising the streets for victims to rob and rape. Over the next few weeks, he burgled homes and boats in Connecticut, stole jewellery, cash, guns and clothes. Off Premium Point in the City of New Rochelle, New York, he broke into a large yacht that was moored a distance off shore and stole a .38 calibre handgun from the galley. When he checked the papers on board, he found that the police commissioner of New Rochelle owned the vessel.

In June 1923, he sailed the yawl up the Hudson River to Yonkers, where he docked overnight. There, he picked up George Walosin, and promised the boy that he could work on the yacht during his trip upriver. On Monday, 25 June 1923, the boat cruised out of the Yonkers dock due north, towards Peekskill, and, later that night, Panzram sodomised the boy. They sailed 50 miles (80.5km) upriver to Kingston, where Panzram moored the yacht in a small bay off the Hudson River.

He quickly repainted the hull and changed the name on the stern. Then he ventured on shore and visited the local hangouts to find a buyer. Soon a young man agreed to come on board to check out the boat, but the man had other things on his mind. 'There he tried to stick me up but I was suspicious of his actions and was ready for him,' Panzram said. He shot the man twice in the head, using the gun that he had stolen from the police commissioner's boat. He then tied a metal weight onto the body and threw the man overboard. 'He's still there yet as far as I know,' Panzram confessed later.

The very next morning, Panzram and his passenger, George Walosin, who had witnessed the killing, sailed out of the bay heading downriver and cruised across to Newburgh.

After the boat dropped anchor, however, George jumped ship and swam to shore, eventually making his way back to Yonkers, where he told the police that he'd been sexually assaulted by Panzram.

Yonkers police alerted all the Hudson River towns to be on the lookout for 'Captain John O'Leary', who was sailing a 38ft (11.6m) yacht downriver. Panzram made it as far as the village of Nyack, where he secured the yawl at Peterson's Boat Yard and bedded down for the night. But, on the morning of 29 June 1923, police boarded the yacht and arrested him. He was charged with sodomy, burglary and robbery. He was placed in the Yonkers city jail awaiting court appearance.

Panzram then turned to his lawyer for help. 'I got a lawyer there, a Mr Cashin. I told him the boat was worth five or ten thousand dollars and that I would give him the boat and the papers if he got me out of jail,' he said. His attorney arranged for bail and a few days later Panzram was released. He never came back. When Cashin went to register the boat, it was discovered that it was stolen. The police immediately confiscated the yacht and Cashin lost the posted bail. Panzram had conned his own lawyer.

After years of murder and rape, Panzram was finally caught, convicted and sentenced to death. At 5.55a.m. on 5 September 1930 he was taken to the gallows of Leavenworth Prison. Asked for any last words, he said that he wished his mother had not brought him into the world. As the executioners assembled Panzram's hood, he hissed at them, 'Hurry up … I could hang a dozen men while you're fooling around …' To various 'do-gooders' who were trying to prevent the execution, he just said, 'I wish you all had one neck and that I had my hands on it!'

# MURDER ON THE *ONEIDA?*

## CALIFORNIA, USA, 1924

On Saturday, 15 November 1924, the newspaper tycoon William Randolph Hearst's 200ft (61m) yacht, *Oneida*, departed from San Pedro, California, on a weekend cruise.

A little jaunt to San Diego was planned in celebration of the movie producer Tom Ince's forty-third birthday. As well as Hearst and Marion Davies, the actress and long-time

Hearst mistress, the ship's crew and a jazz band, there were 15 guests on the yacht that day, including Charlie Chaplin, Dr Daniel Carson Goodman, Cosmopolitan's studio manager, and Louella Parsons. This was Louella's first visit to Hollywood – at that time she was but a mere Hearst movie columnist in New York. Due to pressing commitments, Ince, who was in the final stages of negotiating a production deal with Hearst's International Film Corporation, took a train down the next day and joined the party already in progress.

At dinner on Sunday night the guests celebrated his birthday and early the next morning a water taxi took Ince and Goodman ashore. After boarding a train for Los Angeles, however, Ince fell ill, so they got off the train at Del Mar and checked into a nearby hotel. Goodman called a doctor, who arrived with his nurse. He also phoned Nell Ince, Tom's wife, who immediately headed for Del Mar in her chauffeur-driven car, accompanied by her teenage son. Goodman departed before Nell Ince arrived.

144

Late on Tuesday, Tom Ince died at home. His personal physician signed the death certificate, giving heart failure as the cause of death. To the surprise of Ince's hundreds of friends, employees and admirers, his body was immediately cremated and the memorial service, held the following Friday, was private. Nell Ince soon departed on an extended tour of Europe.

Although Ince was known to suffer from stomach ulcers and angina, gossip that there was something suspicious about his death began to circulate almost immediately, fuelled by a statement issued by the Hearst organisation saying that Ince had fallen ill while visiting Hearst's 'upstate ranch' in the company of his wife and two sons.

The story perplexed colleagues, who knew very well that Ince had been on Hearst's yacht. Why the lie? Although Charlie Chaplin would deny, at times none too convincingly, that he was even present on the *Oneida* that weekend, few believed him. Indeed, the most damaging alleged witness was none other than the normally discreet Toraichi Kono, a loyal Chaplin employee. Kono was present when Ince was brought ashore, and he saw something that upset him – that Ince had been bleeding from a bullet wound to the head.

That William Randolph Hearst shot Ince became part of Hollywood legend. There are two schools of thought on this theory. One dismisses the Ince shooting as a fantasy; the other claims that Hearst had found Marion and Ince together in the yacht's galley late at night. Always supremely possessive of his beloved Marion Davies, this wealthy, yet sad, man had invited Charlie Chaplin along so he could observe the two together. Whispers had come to his ears that Marion and Charlie were more than platonic friends. Ince was looking for something to calm his upset stomach, but Hearst, mistaking him for Chaplin in the poor light, assumed he had walked in on a tryst and shot him. Hearst had thus been aiming at someone else.

It was known that Hearst kept a gun aboard the *Oneida*.

Also, as the famed director D.W. Griffith remarked in later years, 'All you have to do to make Hearst turn white as a ghost is mention Ince's name. There's plenty wrong there, but Hearst is too big to touch.'

Chaplin's comments on Ince's death in his autobiography are equally bizarre. After denying that he was on the *Oneida*, he goes on to say that he, Hearst and Davies visited Ince's bedside together a week after he fell ill. Ince seemed to be improving, Chaplin says, but died two weeks later.

Why would Chaplin, Hearst and Davies have paid a joint call on Ince unless they had all been together on the yacht? On the other hand, why would Chaplin invent such a story? At any rate, Ince survived not three weeks but less than 48 hours. That Friday, Chaplin was a pallbearer at Ince's funeral. On Saturday, he completed the renegotiation of his United Artists contract and on Sunday he departed for Guaymas to reunite with his under-age wife, Lita, whom he was forced marry after she became impregnated.

It was claimed that the gossip queen Louella Parsons earned herself a lifetime contract with the Hearst organisation for keeping quiet about a murder she witnessed.

The mysterious death of Tom Ince was the subject of a film by Peter Bogdanovich called *The Cat's Meow* (2001).

# HOLLYWOOD'S YACHT
## CALIFORNIA, USA, 1935

*Santana* was the brainchild of the son of the founder of the Union Oil Company, W.L. Stewart, Jr, who wanted a schooner that could show her heels to the best and brightest on both the East and West Coasts. Constructed of mahogany planks over white oak frames, she was launched on 24 October 1935. Four years later, *Santana* was bought by Charles Isaacs, a businessman from San Diego married to Eva Gabor, the Hungarian Hollywood actress. *Santana* became the belle of the Hollywood fleet for the next 16 years.

The next owner was the actor George Brent, who converted *Santana* into a yawl before selling her to Ray Milland. Milland owned *Santana* for just three months, fuelling speculation that the movie studios played some role in the ownership of the boat, recognising that it provided a great 'photo opportunity' to gain publicity – a handsome yacht and a leading man. The next owners, the stars Dick Powell and June Allyson, also owned the boat for a very short period before selling her to Humphrey Bogart in 1945.

Bogart, by contrast, was very serious about the boat and was also an excellent helmsman. He explained his purchase of the *Santana* thus: 'An actor needs something to stabilise his personality, something to nail down what he really is, not what he is currently pretending to be.'

Bogart had learned to sail as a child and once he had the

good fortune to own his own boat he sailed her as often as possible, between 35 and 45 weekends a year. Most of those weekends were stag affairs, since Bogie felt that 'the trouble with having dames on board is you can't pee over the side'. In addition to many weekends aboard the boat spent at Catalina, he also did a considerable amount of racing with respectable results. He took first in his class in the San Clemente Island Race of 1950 and first in the 1952 Channel Islands Race.

Bogart and *Santana* played host to many of Hollywood's greatest stars of the time, including Ingrid Bergman, Richard Burton, David Niven and Frank Sinatra.

Niven recalled the night when Sinatra and his party were on a chartered motor yacht nearby. In the evening, Sinatra's boat tied up next to *Santana*, and, accompanied by Jimmy Van Heusen on piano, Sinatra sang all through the night. 'People from other boats rowed over in dinghies and sat in a circle around the two yachts, under a full moon, listening, until the sky began to grow light and the singing ended. Then they rowed quietly away.'

When Bogart wasn't sailing, he still had *Santana* on his mind. When he formed his own production company in 1947, he called it Santana Productions. Bogie starred with Lauren Bacall and Edward G. Robinson in the movie *Key Largo*, and his boat in the film had *Santana* painted on the stern. He also had a complete model of *Santana* on display in his home inside a glass case. When he died, they eulogised the actor, the husband and the father, but it was the model of *Santana*, his love, that stood alongside the pulpit.

After Bogart died *Santana*'s days as a movie star were over. A retired brigadier general raced *Santana* to Hawaii in the Transpac in 1961; in 1966 a wealthy attorney, William Solari, raced her in the 1968 Bermuda Race. In 1971, Charlie Peet, a Sausalito restaurateur, bought *Santana* and sailed her round the world, recalling that everywhere they went they found people who knew the famous boat.

In 1973 M. Lloyd Carter, a 'drama therapist' from Marin County, was also going to sail her around the world, but *Santana* was a wreck and needed extensive repairs. Thomas F. and Theodore A. Eden, twin brothers who ran their own successful architectural firm, finally got the boat back into sailing condition but, in 1993, Tom Eden died and the boat did more sitting than sailing. *Santana* was put up for sale in 1994 and then was withdrawn from the market.

Sometime during the night in November of 1997, *Santana*'s bilge began to fill with water from the bay. It took many hours for the boat to slowly sink in its berth and it wasn't until someone noticed that *Santana*'s decks were nearly awash before anything was done to prevent her from going completely to the bottom of the yacht harbour.

Finally Paul Kaplan, co-owner of Keefe Kaplan Maritime Inc., one of the largest full-service boatyards on San Francisco Bay, and his wife Chrissy discovered her, almost a total wreck, and rescued her. They tore the ceilings out and installed new frames and turned *Santana* back into a schooner. After her relaunch in May 1999, *Santana* was once again the perfect entertainment platform and in classic races she's the schooner to beat.

# RESCUED IN A SANDWICH BOX

## ENGLISH CHANNEL, 1940

The Thames barge *Tollesbury* was named after a fishing village on a tributary of the River Blackwater. In 1901, Tollesbury, Essex, was a loading port for stack barges. Spritsail barges heralded a whole new industry with a special kind of ship and a tough new breed of sailor. The barges were adaptable, fast and economical, typically manned by only three: a skipper, a mate and a boy. They were quick, even in light airs, and the bargemen raced their boats so well that they were recruited as crew for contemporary J-class yachts.

As the *Tollesbury* was built at Sandwich – at Feltham's Yard on the Kentish Stour – and had a squat profile, she was nicknamed *Sandwich Box*. In 1912 she joined the fleet of R. & W. Paul Ltd, the renowned East Anglian wharfingers, who traded in grain, malt and animal feeds. The *Tollesbury* skipper, Lemon Webb, earned his keep – and the *Tollesbury*'s – by carrying stone (from the West Country) and coal, coke and pitch (both ways across the Channel during the First World War). One day at the end of May 1940, Lemon Webb was sailing his ship up the Thames near Erith when a naval launch came alongside with instructions: proceed to Cory's jetty for orders. At the jetty, Lem Webb and his 19-year-old lad were given a choice: leave the ship or volunteer to help evacuate the British Expeditionary Force from Dunkirk. Both immediately agreed to go forth with the *Tollesbury*. By

2p.m. they were part of a flotilla of pleasure-boats, fireboats, tugs and barges, including the *Ethel Everard* of London, towed by the tug *Sun XI*.

The plan was to sacrifice the barges by beaching them so the troops could use them as embarkation platforms. Then the soldiers could be transferred to small boats and launches, and eventually to the larger boats lying in deep water. The barges' wooden hulls would protect them from magnetic mines, and their flat bottoms meant they could go closer in than other craft. Lemon Webb had orders to beach his craft.

The *Tollesbury* arrived at midnight and was abandoned by her tug. As there was little wind, Webb and his lad used their 'sweeps' (24ft (7.3m) long oars) to get close to the shore. On hearing the shouts of soldiers ashore, warning them of the shallows, they let go their anchor. But attempts to provide access for the troops across a wooden ladder failed when a surge broke the ladder. Instead they provided a makeshift gangway by lowering their tender.

Then 273 soldiers came aboard.

The soldiers were wet, sunburned, exhausted and desperate for food and water. Lemon Webb gladly provided them with water, biscuits and a few loaves of bread.

The next problem was relaunching the *Tollesbury*, which had grounded with the falling tide. It was two hours before the tide refloated the barge. They pushed off into deep water, setting their sails, but they made little progress in the light winds. So they dropped anchor again and the mate, a First World War navy veteran, signalled a destroyer and asked for the troops to be transferred. First, the *Tollesbury* had to survive an air raid. Then a barge tried to tow them off too quickly and the towline snapped.

When they finally set sail for Ramsgate, they were subjected to another air raid, bombs dropping within feet of the barge while a destroyer and torpedo boat drove off the attackers. During their voyage they saw two destroyers sink and narrowly avoided an exploding mine near the North Goodwins.

At Ramsgate Roads they transferred their passengers to motorboats to be taken ashore.

'She is a lucky ship, skipper!' said one grateful soldier.

Indeed the *Tollesbury* continued to survive. Having had a diesel engine fitted, she served as houseboat at Pin Mill, Suffolk, until the early 1990s. Then she was rebuilt in Ipswich and moved to Docklands, where she passed her one-hundredth birthday as a bar-diner! The *Tollesbury*'s menu had come a long way from Lemon Webb's tiny portions of water, biscuits and bread.

Ironically, given her history, she was bombed and damaged by the IRA in 1996. She was repaired but sunk in 2005 before being raised and moved to a mooring in Barking. Euan Maybank and his partner Rachael Smith had been looking for a boat to live on when they spotted the *Tollesbury* for sale in 2011. 'I wasn't convinced when we first saw her,' admitted Rachael, 28, 'as she needed a lot of work and was all black inside. But Euan got it into his head that we should buy her and after a while I came around. It felt right.'

'We hope to sail her, maybe within a couple of years, if we can get all the necessary work done,' said Euan. 'We have motored her which was fantastic, but having the sails up would be a very different experience. I can't wait for that day.'

# DUNKIRK'S LITTLE *ENA*
## ENGLISH CHANNEL, 1940

Six of the 16 barges that sailed to Dunkirk were owned by the wharfingers R. & W. Paul. One of them was the *Ena*. She was rigged as a 'mulie' – a compromise between a more substantial ketch and a spritsail barge. She had a tall mizzenmast, a large gaff sail (well forward of the wheel) and a smaller spritsail.

R. & W. Paul had supported the armed forces on other occasions. During the First World War, when Paul's barges had acted as supply ships in Europe, it was common to see a hundred barges loading and unloading in Boulogne and Dieppe. Their small draught gave them access to shallow waters, they were less likely to be sunk by mines and German U-boat captains were often reluctant to show themselves, or even to waste a precious torpedo, by attacking a mere sailing barge.

In 1940, the *Ena* survived her initial 100 mile (161km) outward journey across the mine-strewn English Channel. After evading constant air attacks, Alfred Page, the skipper, was ordered to beach the *Ena* close to the smaller sand barge *H.A.C.* As the Germans closed in, the crews of both barges were ordered to abandon their boats and escape on a minesweeper to England. Alex Smith was one of 30 men of the Duke of Wellington's Regiment commanded by Captain David Strangeways, their adjutant. Smith later recalled how they arrived on La Panne beach and could not believe their luck when they saw two seaworthy barges anchored and almost afloat. They took possession of the *H.A.C.* while Colonel McKay and the 19th Field Regiment, Royal Artillery, boarded the nearby *Ena*.

Captain Atley of the East Yorks Regiment and one of his men made a raft. Using shovels, they rowed out to the *Ena*. They helped 36 other men on board, including three wounded, and the *Ena* set sail at 8a.m.

Then, according to Alex Smith, the two ships got involved in one of the most remarkable barge races of all time. Under constant enemy bombardment and machine-gun fire, they sped across the Channel.

Atley later recalled that at midnight, when they took a back-bearing on Dunkirk, they found they had gone too far southwest. Atley's only sailing experience had been on the Broads and he had forgotten to put the leeboards down. So they changed course to north-northwest and finally sighted the North Goodwin buoy. They then had to tack again towards the South Goodwin Lightship.

Eventually, a tug or fleet auxiliary took the *Ena* into Margate. As the harbour was full, the empty barge was then towed out and left anchored off Deal.

The R. & W. Paul shipping manager had presumed the *Ena* lost on the Dunkirk beaches. He was amazed to learn that the barge was lying off Deal. Skipper Page, by then back in Ipswich, was sent to recover her.

The *Ena* was seaworthy but had been stripped of all her gear. 'They had taken the sweeps, mooring lines, fenders and even my false teeth which I had left behind in a glass of water by my bunk!' Page said. 'You can't trust these men of Kent!'

In 1974 the Ena was transferred to the Social and Sports Club of Paul's in Ipswich and she was still competing in the 1990s in sailing barge races on the Thames, the Medway, Blackwater and Orwell, keeping the great tradition of the spritsail barges alive.

# THE OLD MEN OF THE SEA

## CUBA, 1942

Two of Ernest Hemingway's most endearing characters, Antonio, from *Islands in the Stream*, and Santiago, from *The Old Man and the Sea*, were modelled after Gregorio Fuentes, Hemingway's closest friend, confidant and the captain of his custom-built fishing yacht, *Pilar*, for the last 30 years of the writer's life.

The sea had played an integral part in Fuentes's life. He was born on 11 July 1897 in the Canary Islands. His mother, Sebastiana Betancourt, was a housewife, his father, Pedro, a labourer on a cargo ship. The younger Fuentes's first adventure at sea, at the tender age of six, had tragic consequences. While he was on a voyage with his father from the Canary Islands to the West Indies to deliver potato seeds, the elder Fuentes was crushed to death by a falling mast.

Fuentes's first meeting with the future literary giant was an accident and an adventure. The 25-year-old Fuentes, then captain of a fishing vessel making regular trips between Cuba and the US mainland in the 1920s, was returning from Cuba when he noticed a stranded boat, out of fuel, several miles off the Florida coast. When the occupant of the boat called out for help in Spanish, Fuentes came to the rescue.

'As I approached the boat, the man who spoke such beautiful Spanish, said that he was American. That was Mr Hemingway,' Fuentes says. 'Mr Hemingway said that he was very hungry because he had been stranded for a long period of time without food. So I shared the onions and wine that we had on board with him.'

Fuentes towed Hemingway and his boat to a lighthouse in the US Dry Tortugas. The last thing Hemingway said that day to the young Cuban was, 'Goodbye, my friend. I'll see you again in Cuba.'

That prophecy proved true several years later. When he was introduced to Ernest Hemingway in a café they recognised each other immediately and Hemingway offered Fuentes a job as captain of his fishing yacht, *Pilar*. A friendship lasting more than 30 years was forged.

In 1942, the boat had been crewed by eight of Hemingway's most trusted cronies, including Fuentes, who loaded her with grenades, high-calibre machine guns – disassembled and sneaked on board in people's pockets – bazookas, short-fuse bombs, a collapsible rubber dinghy for emergencies, and sound-detection gear.

She had then served as a Q-boat hunting German submarines, which were torpedoing Allied tankers off Cuba and along the eastern coast of the United States. Hemingway had sought and got reluctant official permission for his plan from Colonel Thomason, chief of Naval Intelligence for Central America. Thomason broke all military regulations to procure the necessary equipment. For about a year and a half, *Pilar* cruised the Gulf Stream and the islands off Cuba's north coast, a month at a time, pretending to be a scientific expeditionary ship, in a fruitless search for U-boats before the project was disbanded.

In 1951, Hemingway produced a story that would win him the 1953 Pulitzer Prize and the 1954 Nobel Prize for Literature. *The Old Man and the Sea* told the tale of an old Cuban fisherman who spent four days fighting a swordfish only to lose it to sharks. Fuentes later recalled the moment when Hemingway had lighted upon his subject:

'One afternoon on the high seas off the Cuban port of

Cabanas, we came across a boat with an old fisherman and a young boy on board, trying to save a marlin they had just caught from the sharks attacking it. We tried to help and the fisherman responded by insulting us. Mr Hemingway told me not to pay any attention to him, and said he probably thought we were trying to steal the fish from him.'

Hemingway later bequeathed his old friend a free meal and a free Havana cigar at La Terraza restaurant every day for the rest of his life. He also asked Fuentes to take care of *Pilar*.

After Hemingway's suicide in 1961, Fuentes never took the boat out again and eventually turned it over to Fidel Castro's revolutionary government. Today, the *Pilar* is dry-docked at the Hemingway Museum in San Francisco de Paula, a national monument. Fuentes died on 13 January 2002 at the age of 104.

# POON LIM'S
# ENDURING LEGACY
## SOUTHERN ATLANTIC, 1942

On 23 November 1942, the British merchant ship SS *Ben Lomond* was hit by a torpedo from a German U-boat and sank within minutes. As the crew scrambled to launch the ship's lifeboats, Second Steward Poon Lim took matters into his own hands and flung himself from the listing ship into the icy waters of the Atlantic. A poor swimmer, Lim managed to grab a lifebelt and he paddled about desperately, hoping to encounter his colleagues. Strong currents, however, carried him away from the boat and the other survivors in their lifeboats, and he was soon alone on the vast ocean 565 miles (909km) west of St Paul's Rocks on the Equator, above the eastern tip of Brazil. It was the start of an incredible saga of endurance and courage.

After a few hours, Lim came across a wooden raft and manage to scramble onto it. There he found some tins of biscuits, a bag of sugar lumps and some chocolate, a flask of water, plus flares, smoke pots and a flashlight. For the next four months, however, these meagre supplies would be all he had to sustain him as he drifted with the currents. The water and the food on the raft were exhausted, and Poon's problems began in earnest. Because he was a poor swimmer, he regularly had to tie himself to the raft by his wrist in case, during a large swell, he fell into the ocean.

Where drinking water was concerned, he utilised the canvas life jacket he had snatched just before leaping to safety to trap rainwater. As for fishing, he made a rudimentary fish-hook using a wire from the flashlight and used a hemp rope as a fishing line. For catching larger fish, he prised a nail out of the boards of the wooden raft and bent it into a hook. When he managed to land a fish, he would cut it open with a knife he created from a biscuit tin and dry it on a hemp line erected over the raft. It was a struggle against ever-threatening elements, however, as storms regularly spoiled his fish and fouled his water. At one point, barely alive, Poon somehow managed to catch a bird and drink its blood.

His resourcefulness knew no bounds. Unfazed by the sight of sharks circling his raft, he set out to catch one using the remnants of a bird he'd caught as bait. The shark that took the bait was just a few feet long but almost broke the line as it struggled to get free. Poon had taken the precaution of braiding the line so it would have double thickness and also wrapping his hands in canvas to enable him to grapple with the animal. In fact, the shark attacked him as he brought it aboard the raft but Lim used the water jug half-filled with seawater as a weapon. He stunned it before sucking its blood in order to quench his thirst. He then sliced the fins – considered a Cantonese delicacy – and let them dry in the sun.

Being so far out in the ocean, the chance of being picked up by a passing ship was remote, although he was seen twice, first by a German U-boat, which had been doing gunnery drills by targeting seagulls, and later by an unidentified freighter. The latter passed him by, Poon later contended, because the crew, seeing that he was Asian, thought he was a survivor from a sunken Japanese warship.

There was also a squad of US Navy patrol planes who spotted him, one dropping a marker buoy in the water. Unfortunately for Poon, a large storm hit the area almost simultaneously and he was lost again.

At last, on the morning of 5 April 1943, Poon caught the attention of some fishermen plying their trade some

10 miles (16.1km) off the coast of Brazil. They saw Poon waving a shirt and jumping about, turned their boat around and picked him up.

Poon's 133-day ordeal at sea alone on a raft is a record for a lone human. When told no one had ever survived longer, he replied, 'I hope no one will ever have to break that record.'

Despite his trying ordeal during which he lost 20lb (9.1kg) in body weight, Poon was able to walk ashore unaided when he arrived at Salinopolis, Brazil. He spent four weeks in hospital before returning to Britain where he was awarded the British Empire Medal. Poon died in Brooklyn, USA, on 4 January 1991, after becoming an American citizen. His legend lives on however. The Royal Navy has included his amazing tale into its survival technique manuals, while the acclaimed science fiction writer, Alfred Bester, drew on Poon Lim's nightmare experience in his novel *The Stars My Destination*, which opens with a man stranded in space …

# THE YACHTS IN ERROL FLYNN'S LIFE (AND DEATH)

## CALIFORNIA, USA, 1942; FRENCH RIVIERA, 1970s

In the spring of 1938 Errol Flynn saw a picture of a boat in *Yachting* magazine: a John Alden classic, 75ft (22.9m) ketch that had just been built in Boston – sleek, shiny and made for adventure. He named it *Sirocco* and, as a yacht owner, Flynn greatly increased his social standing in Southern California. He luxuriated in long, leisurely, spring voyages down the coves and bays meeting people who had become his peers: John Ford, the famous director in his 110ft (33.5m) ketch, the *Araner*; fellow actor James Cagney on the *Martha*; Harry Cohn, the movie mogul of Columbia Pictures, aboard his *Gem of the Breakwater*.

However, in December 1942, the idyll was shattered when Flynn was arrested on a double charge of statutory rape. Teenager Betty Hansen claimed he had taken advantage of her at a friend's home while 16-year-old Peggy Satterlee placed *her* seduction on board Flynn's yacht, the *Sirocco*.

The scandalous trial entertained a war-weary public during 1943 with sensational stories of Flynn's sex- and booze-soaked escapades with all his sexual indiscretions exposed to a prurient public.

The rape had allegedly taken place on a boat trip to Catalina Island during the weekend of 1–3 August 1941. During his trial, Flynn testified that he could not have had sex with Peggy Satterlee because 'entertainment' would have been the *last* thing on his mind on that trip: not only had he been mourning the recent death of a close friend but, on an earlier sailing trip to Balboa, his beloved Schnauzer, Arno, had gone overboard.

The dog had developed a habit of snapping after flying fish. At night, Arno was normally locked up in the galley, where he had a spacious kennel and a variety of large bones. But, on the night voyage from San Pedro to Balboa, Arno had apparently slipped his leash and made his way up a companionway to the deck while the watch was sleeping on duty. Spying a fish, the dog had jumped up and fallen into the sea.

Flynn had woken at dawn and checked the vessel as usual. When he looked in the kennel, he was shocked to find Arno missing. He began whistling and calling but there was no responsive bark. He began to panic. He woke the crew and searched the cabins. But there was no sign of Arno. Realising what must have happened, he burst into tears.

After docking in Balboa, Flynn went to the harbourmaster. The whole available fleet was put out to sea to search for the missing dog but by nightfall Arno had not been found. Flynn went out on the *Sirocco*, pacing the deck, training binoculars on the sea. Three days later, Arno's remains were washed ashore a few miles down the coast. Flynn took the collar, and would later bury it in the tiny animal graveyard under the walls of his house on Mulholland Drive. Members of the Coast Guard staged a replica of a naval burial, shipping the dog out to sea in a tiny coffin and slipping it off the deck under the Stars and Stripes by moonlight at dead of night.

In fact, Arno had drowned some time *after* the Catalina 'rape' trip. What's more, the dog was clearly on board during the entire voyage, visible in a number of the pictures taken by various show-business magazines.

Nevertheless, an all-female jury acquitted him and Flynn's movie bosses tried briefly to polish up his image with various superhero roles. Unfortunately, Flynn had lost his youthful sparkle. The ageing rebel creaked on through a decade of flabby parts in forgettable films before dying of a heart attack aged 50 in the arms of a 17-year-old girlfriend.

Legend has it, erroneously, that he died on his last yacht, the *Zaca*, a 118ft (36m) schooner. The name means 'peace' in Samoan. The famous newscaster Walter Cronkite's widow, Betsy, had the last word: 'Errol Flynn died on a 70-foot [21.3m] boat with a 17-year-old girl. Walter has always wanted to go that way, but he's going to settle for a 17-footer with a 70-year-old.'

In fact, Flynn parted with the *Zaca* only after a period of illness and financial difficulties. While at a party, Flynn complained that he was tired and that he needed to lie down. On the way to the hosts' bedroom, he suffered his heart attack and died. Flynn's death was a sad affair. Not only was his funeral sparsely attended by his friends, but his grave went unmarked for some 20 years after his death in 1959. After his demise, misfortune plagued his loved ones.

What's more, the *Zaca* broke down after Flynn's death and was moored in the French Riviera. While the schooner lay rotting in a shipyard, the ghost of the matinée idol was seen pacing the deck on several occasions. After seeing Flynn's apparition, a watchman jumped ship and was pulled from the water in a state of shock. Another eyewitness heard a spectral party being held aboard the yacht, and saw lights flashing on and off – strange, since the ship was deserted and devoid of electricity.

The owners of the shipyard decided to restore the *Zaca* during the 1970s. However, because of the paranormal activity, they decided that an exorcism was needed to lay Flynn's ghost to rest. Rather than hold the exorcism aboard the yacht itself, a 30in (76.2cm) long model was built and taken to a church to be used in the ceremony. Several people who had encountered the spirit took part in the ritual, which was presided over by a Catholic priest and an Anglican archdeacon.

After the exorcism, those present felt that Flynn's spirit had finally 'crossed over'.

# THE *LEOPOLDVILLE* DISASTER

## ENGLISH CHANNEL, 1944

On Christmas Eve 1944, the Belgian troopship SS *Leopoldville*, only 5 miles (8km) from its destination and loaded with more than 2,000 American soldiers, was struck by a German torpedo off the coast of Cherbourg, France.

One missile struck the ship below the water line on the starboard side, towards the stern. The blast left a gaping hole in the hull and survivors recall seeing debris and bodies violently tossed into the air. Many soldiers, roused from sleep by the thunderous explosion, were at first unaware of the gravity of the situation. Shock turned to mayhem, as men stumbled and groped in the darkness amid the screams of the wounded as tons of ice-cold seawater rushed into the holds.

The ship listed for about two hours. Many men clung to the rails and literally slid off the upraised bow before the ship went down in a whirlpool of bubbles, its suction taking many victims with her.

By Christmas Day morning, nearly 800 young men, most between the ages of 18 and 21, were dead in the 48°F (8.9°C) Channel waters. They represented soldiers from 47 of the then 48 American states; 650 were injured; 493 bodies were never found.

The first explosion took 100 lives. Others were crushed or trapped under collapsed decks; but too many others perished through a series of cruel blunders.

The soldiers had received only one drill: to assemble on deck in case of an emergency. No lifeboat, fire or abandon-ship drills had been held on board and they were not instructed in how to lower lifeboats or free life rafts. The 2,625 life jackets were issued haphazardly, if at all, without instruction.

Many of the 238 Belgian crewmen under Commander Charles Limbour took to the lifeboats after the torpedo struck. It was claimed they made no efforts, except for taking 30 stretcher cases with them, to help the soldiers get off in the remaining lifeboats or to cut the lashing of rafts and floater nets secured on deck.

Many men were crushed to death in doomed attempts to leap from the sinking troopship onto the British destroyer HMS *Brilliant*, which had pulled up alongside in the tossing, dark sea. In doing so, it smashed many lifeboats to smithereens.

Tragically, lack of proper life-preserver training proved fatal to many men. You're supposed to cross your arms over your chest, so that when you hit the water the life preserver won't snap up and snap your neck. Many rescuers found bodies in the water with broken necks.

In order to hide the magnitude of the calamity, the US Army staggered death notifications between January and April 1945. In what can only be seen as a cruel hoax, families were sent telegrams reporting their son was 'missing in action', when the army knew full well the men were dead. Months later, those same families received a second telegram, confirming their worst fears.

# ORWELL AND THE WHIRLPOOL

## SCOTLAND, 1947

The Corryvreckan Whirlpool is the stuff of legend. The third largest in the world, it occurs in the Gulf of Corryvreckan, which separates the Inner Hebridean Isle of Jura from the island of Scarba on Scotland's west coast. When the whirlpool is in full motion, the half-mile (0.8km) wide channel is a very dangerous place to be. Currents can reach 16 knots (29.6km/h), waves 10ft (3m) high break endlessly and its roar can be heard 10 miles (16.1km) away.

Tales of boats being caught in it and sucked down into the depths of the monster make it perhaps the most feared strip of water around Britain's coast; the Royal Navy has classed the channel as unnavigable, and the local lifeboat has been called out to more than 50 emergencies in recent years.

In 1947, George Orwell (whose real name was Eric Arthur Blair), took a short break from writing his novel *Nineteen Eighty-Four*, which would be published two years later. To complete the book, Orwell had taken a home on Jura. That summer, he invited his young nieces and nephews, including three-year-old Ricky, out for a boating expedition. Unexpectedly, they came upon the infamous Corryvreckan Whirlpool and disaster soon struck.

Orwell's nephew Henry Dakin has recalled that, as they turned round the point, there was already a fair swell. The boat was rising and falling, but they weren't worried because Orwell seemed to know what he was doing. He had spent a lot of time mending and caulking the boat and it had an outboard motor, but as they came round the point they saw that the whirlpool had not receded.

The famous Corryvreckan was not just the one big whirlpool, but had a lot of smaller whirlpools around the edges, and, before they had a chance to turn, they went straight into the minor whirlpools and lost control. Orwell was at the tiller, and, according to Dakin, 'the boat went all over the place, pitching and tossing, very frightening being thrown from one small whirlpool to another, pitching and tossing so much that the outboard motor jerked right off from its fixing.'

Orwell then said, very calmly and flatly, 'The motor's gone, better get the oars out, Hen. Can't help much, I'm afraid.' He was sitting at the back of the boat, and wasn't particularly strong, so Dakin unshipped the oars and, partly with the current and partly with the oars, but mostly with the current, tried to steady the boat and make for a little rock island.

As they got close to the island, the boat was rising and falling about 12ft (3.7m) on the swell. Dakin had taken off his boots in case he had to swim but, as the boat rose level with the island, he jumped round with the painter – the mooring rope – in his hand onto the sharp rocks, hurting his feet. He turned to see that the boat had fallen down and, though he still had his hand on the painter, the boat had turned upside down.

First Lucy appeared, then Orwell appeared and cried out, 'I've got Ricky all right.' He had grabbed the boy as the boat had turned over and pulled him out from under it. He then had to swim from the end of the boat to the side of the island, still hanging onto the boy, but he managed, according to Dakin, to keep his normal 'Uncle Eric' face the whole time, without panicking. Eventually they were all able to clamber up onto the island.

They were now left on an island about 100 yards (91.4m) long with the boat, one oar, a fishing rod and their clothes. Orwell got his cigarette lighter out and put it out on a rock to dry. They hadn't been there three minutes, however, when he said he would go off and find some food. 'A slightly ridiculous thing, it struck me afterwards,' Dakin recalled, 'because we had had breakfast only two hours before and the last thing that any of us was thinking of was eating or of hunger. When he came back, the first thing he said was, "Puffins are curious birds, they live in burrows. I saw some baby seagulls, but I haven't the heart to kill them."'

'I thought we were goners,' Orwell said, almost seeming to enjoy it. They attached a shirt to the fishing rod and waved it about, and after about an hour and a half a lobster boat spotted them and picked them up with some difficulty, because the fisherman could not come up close to the island because of the swell and had to throw a rope across. They clambered along the rope one by one, Orwell taking Ricky on his back.

Dakin concluded, 'The lobsterman landed us at the north of the island and we just walked about a quarter of an hour or 20 minutes and came across Avril and Jane working hard hoeing in a field. They said to us, "What took you so long?"'

# SIMON THE CAT AND THE 'YANGTZE INCIDENT'

## CHINA, 1949

In 1949, as the civil war between the opposing Chinese Communists under Mao Tse-tung and Chiang Kai-shek's Nationalists drew to a close, the destroyer HMS *Consort* was standing as guard ship to the British Embassy in Nanking, ready to evacuate the staff and other British nationals if necessary. As the *Consort* was running low on fuel, the *Amethyst*, a Black Swan Class sloop, was ordered to proceed up the Yangtze River to Nanking and replace her.

It was not seriously expected that the Communists would attack the ship but at 9.20a.m., as the frigate approached the village of San-Chiang-ying, a battery opened up. The slaughter was almost unimaginable, blood flowing across the deck into the scuppers. Seventeen men were soon dead and 25 were seriously wounded.

Realising the gravity of their situation, officers ordered the immediate evacuation of most of the crew. A stand-off ensued while negotiations took place.

At the time of the initial attack, Simon – a green-eyed, black-and-white tom – was asleep in the captain's cabin when it took a direct hit. He was thrown into the air and landed heavily, lying motionless on a debris-strewn gangway.

Amid the human carnage, Simon was picked up and carried below. His whiskers and eyebrows had been burned off, and his singed fur was matted with grime and the blood from numerous shell splinter gashes to his back and both his left legs. The shards of metal were carefully removed from his wounds, and he was made as comfortable as possible, even though nobody expected him to last the night.

Simon, however, made a miraculous recovery, surviving that first night when he had been expected to join the list of fatalities, and, though still severe, his wounds started to heal. It was not a moment too soon. Disturbed by the shelling, hordes of rats had started to raid the ship's dwindling food supplies and were even invading the sleeping quarters.

Negotiations with the Communists for the ship's release dragged on unprofitably, because the Chinese wanted an admission that the *Amethyst* had fired first – which was continually refused because it was patently untrue. Life on board became hot, humid and boring.

As the crewmen tried to rest in the increasingly stifling heat, the rats were literally nibbling at their toes. When Simon caught his first large rat, the boost to the crew's morale was unimaginable.

While Simon showed no mercy with the rats, he was often to be found comforting his shipmates and, along with Peggy, the ship's four-year-old terrier (with whom he apparently got on well), he provided a vital focus for reminding the men of the domesticity of home some thought they might never see again. Finally, on the night of 30 July 1949, *Amethyst* left under cover of darkness, and, after a further series of adventures, and more damage from Communist guns on shore, made it to the open sea.

The ordeal was over, after 101 days. King George VI sent his congratulations and ordered that the mainbrace be spliced. Simon was immediately recommended for the People's Dispensary for Sick Animals Dickin Medal for acts of bravery in wartime by animals serving with the police, Civil Defence or any branch of the armed forces. Not only was he the first – and so far the only – cat to gain the medal, but it was the first time a Royal Navy animal had received it. A special collar in the colours of the medal ribbon was sent for Simon to wear, and he was due to be presented with the actual medal upon his return to the UK.

On 1 November the *Amethyst* sailed into Plymouth Harbour to a tumultuous welcome, but while the crew were reunited with family and friends, Simon was packed off to quarantine kennels in Surrey. On 28 November, Simon died. He had been born with a weak heart, and his wounds and frequent battles with oversized rats had finally taken their toll.

A few days later, his body wrapped in cotton wool and his tiny coffin draped with a Union Jack, Simon was laid to rest in plot 281 of the PDSA's pet cemetery in Ilford, Essex, with full naval honours.

In 1950, the American author Paul Gallico dedicated his novel *Jennie* simply, 'To the late Simon, of the *Amethyst*'.

# ADRIAN HAYTER'S MYSTERIOUS LIGHT

## DJIBUTI, INDIAN OCEAN, 1950s

In 1950, Adrian Hayter resigned his commission in a Gurkha regiment, sank his savings into a 32ft (9.7m) yawl, *Sheila II*, and with little experience of the sea set out to sail from England to his birthplace, Nelson, in New Zealand. It would be six long years before he made his final landfall. A few years later, in 1963, he would become one of the select band of intrepid single-handed circumnavigators using a folkboat called *Sheila* and another tiny boat, the *Valkyri*.

During the countless, lonely days at sea, Hayter encountered and overcame numerous seaborne hazards, including a cyclone, sailing through a minefield, suffering from exposure and starvation and being becalmed in the Doldrums. But nothing spooked him more than a strange occurrence off the coast of Africa on an altogether more benign trip, this time with a fellow yachtsman.

They were sailing in his favourite boat, *Sheila*, and were close to the Djibuti Lighthouse off the East African coast, but, owing to light winds, they did not sight the lighthouse on its guardian coral reefs until dusk on the second evening.

Although he had no large-scale chart, the pilot book gave detailed instructions for entry, so, as the reefs could be avoided in the darkness by bearings from the various lights, he decided to go in that night rather than wait for dawn.

As night fell softly and *Sheila* was sailing herself gently across a warm breeze, Hayter and his companion were talking in the cockpit when they noticed a light far out to the southeast. It pivoted in the south, and swept from one horizon to the other. As they watched, it seemed to grow more vivid and they sensed it was sweeping towards them like the beam of a very powerful lighthouse – but this light was *under the water*!

The inexplicable light rapidly came closer until it lit up the sails with a greenish luminescence bright enough, according to Hayter, to read by. He watched transfixed as the beam then passed under *Sheila*, throwing the dark shadow of her hull momentarily over the sails, before it fled to the western horizon. It left the two men speechless, but then another great beam appeared in the east, swung towards them again, swept underneath the boat, and silently fled into the western darkness.

This happened five times, in exactly the same way, at the same regular intervals, in complete silence and with no change in the wind or sea. Hayter remarked later that his friend, although a devout atheist, 'uttered a shaking blasphemy, and admitted that one more beam would have put him on his knees'.

There has never been any suitable explanation for the weird and fascinating phenomenon Hayter witnessed.

# CAUGHT IN THE NETS
## IRISH SEA, 1954

The Boeing B-29 Superfortress was a four-engine, propeller-driven heavy bomber, flown primarily by the United States during the Second World War and the Korean War. It was one of the largest operational aircraft and very advanced for its time. In fact, one of the B-29's final roles during the Second World War was carrying out the atomic bomb attacks on Hiroshima and Nagasaki. The RAF flew the B-29 as the Washington until phasing out the type in 1954. In that same year, on 26 January over Morecambe Bay, a B-29 crashed in the sea in a blizzard – all seven members of the crew were posted as missing.

On 1 February at 7.40p.m., the 203-ton fishing trawler *Nellie Melling* was operating off Maughold Head, the eastern-most point of the Isle of Man. As the crew hauled in at the end of a long day, however, they made a grim discovery – entangled in the nets amid the fish and the seaweed was the body of an airman dressed in full flying gear and with an unopened parachute harnessed to his back.

The men had little time in which to react, however. Fifty-year-old skipper Harry Buckley told them, 'in no uncertain terms', to throw the dead airman back into the sea.

Crewman Kenneth Robinson, himself an ex-RAF Sergeant air-gunner said, 'As an ex-RAF man I felt strongly about it.' In fact, the men insisted that the body should be brought ashore 'for a Christian burial'. They protested in vain. The skipper was adamant. One of the crew later explained, 'The skipper told us the best thing we could do was to forget it. He said: "We have disturbed him from his grave and have now put him back."'

Douglas Wilkes, 28, another deckhand on the *Nellie Melling*, later told reporters, 'On the trip we signed a protest. The skipper didn't even give us sufficient time to collect proper evidence from the airman's clothing and equipment to establish his identity.' Later, Wilkes found a wristlet watch in the net. The watch had stopped at 12.20a.m. – about the time shortly after midnight when the Washington bomber was believed to have crashed in the sea.

An Air Ministry official in London told a *Northern Daily Mail* reporter the next day: 'The body is still not identified, but investigations are going on.' The official added, however, that they hoped the type of parachute pack the airman was wearing would help them make a 'shortlist' of possible men.

Another member of the crew also told reporters that the service number of a glove found on the body had been noted. RAF officials, however, found that the number did not tally with that of any member of the lost Washington bomber.

All of which simply added to the anguish of Mrs Vera Johnston, 21-year-old widow of Wishford Road, Grangetown, Sunderland. Her husband, Sergeant Air Gunner George Johnston, had been one of the missing aircrew. The deckhands on the *Nellie Melling* all testified that the man in the nets had a shock of black hair, similar to Johnston's. Air Force officials conceded that Sergeant Johnston or another member of the crew might have been wearing borrowed gloves.

Skipper Buckley, however, when interviewed later would not comment on the crew's protest ('I'm making no statement to the press') but said, 'They had plenty of opportunity to get identification. I am in charge of the vessel and she was on the high seas.'

Five of the original crew refused to sign on with the trawler after she docked at Fleetwood. They were later joined by two more of their shipmates. The following day it was reported that it took four hours to recruit enough men from the seamen's pool to make up a full crew for the *Nellie Melling*, which was due to sail on the afternoon tide.

# RIDING ALONG ON THE CREST OF A WAVE

## ATLANTIC OCEAN, 1954

For two hours in a raging Atlantic gale, Christopher Brinsmead, a 19-year-old oil-tanker apprentice racked with cramp, clung desperately to a lifebuoy. The ship from which he had been swept – the 9,000-ton tanker *Mactra* – had disappeared, and the nearest land was 36 miles (60km) away. To Christopher, lashed by the stinging spray and rain in the bitter cold with 60ft (18.3m) waves breaking around him, his leg injured, his fingers clawing at the lifebuoy, the position seemed hopeless.

But he survived.

'Fortunately one of the watchmen on the bridge had seen me go overboard. He threw two lifebelts. One fell a hundred yards [91.4m] away,' he said later. Christopher, already blue with cold, kicked off his sea-boots and swam desperately towards it. But by the time the *Mactra* stopped Christopher had disappeared. He was hidden by the rain-squalls and in the deep troughs of the waves. For more than an hour the ship searched.

'I was getting desperate. I had the cramp and every time a wave broke over me I was swallowing water. I thought I would never see land again. I didn't think I could hold on much longer. I began to wonder just what it would be like to drown.'

Then through the rain he saw a ship. She was 1 mile (1.6km) away.

'I started to shout and wave but it was no good, they couldn't see me.' By now the cramp was almost unbearable. He was going under with every wave.

Then, miraculously, Christopher, with the tiny lifebelt round his middle, was tossed high on the crest of a wave. Across the boiling seas came a blast of the ship's siren. They had seen him. 'I never heard a more wonderful sound in my life,' he said. But even then his nightmare was not over. So severe was the storm that it was impossible to launch a boat. Steaming as near to him as they could the crew of the *Mactra* prepared to fire a lifeline by rocket. The first missed. The second sent a line snaking over his head. 'It was all I could do to grab it. I clung on like grim death and they began to haul me in.'

# HAMMOND INNES'S INSPIRATION

## ENGLISH CHANNEL, 1956

Hammond Innes was an English adventure author who wrote more than 30 novels, producing books in a regular sequence of six months of travel and research and then six months of writing. Many featured the sea.

In his classic tale, *The Wreck of the Mary Deare*, John Sands is the captain of a salvage ship that is almost rammed by the apparently abandoned *Mary Deare*. Sands boards the ship in search of plunder but, as it is tossed on the high seas, he discovers the half-crazed first mate of the *Mary Deare*, Gideon Patch, who tells Sands a tale of sabotage, robbery and conspiracy, masterminded by other members of the crew. In the end the ship is scuttled and sinks. While Sands believes the story, the court does not, and Patch is devastated. Determined to prove his innocence, the two captains dive down to the sunken *Mary Deare* to dredge up the evidence they need, leading to a thrilling climax. Innes was a keen sailor, and claimed that the inspiration for *The Wreck of the Mary Deare* came when he and a fellow yachtsman were sailing off Omonville-la-Rogue near Cherbourg in the English Channel. It was well after dark and, because it was an open anchorage with no leading lights, they decided to stand off and on until dawn. They went into one-man watches of two hours each, looking forward to an early-morning run ashore before sailing round Cap de la Hague, then westward into Brittany.

The wind was lightish, about force three, and it was very dark. They sailed alternately one hour to the south, one hour to the north, their speed through the water barely 4 knots (7.4km/h).

At 2a.m. Innes was relieved at the helm. There was a chill in the air and he was wearing oilskins. As he came up through the hatch, he shifted the tiller, leaning back to the roll of the boat, and saw, past him over the stern, a glimmer of luminosity. He was still half asleep but recalled that his heart gave a jump, for the luminosity was spreading, lighting up the swell. It was a green luminosity, and in his half-awake state he saw it suddenly as the phosphorescent glow of some deep-sea monster surfacing close behind them. 'What the hell's that?' he recalled, pointing.

The light had grown from a glimmer to a ghostly glow that lit the sea and the air. His companion, George, turned and stared aft. Neither of them spoke.

The light began to change: from all-pervading green it hardened very slowly into a pinpoint. And then they heard it, the rumble of a ship's engines, and in that instant George grabbed the spotlight and shone it on their sails to show whoever was on the ship's bridge that they were there.

The night above them filled with a white, iridescent glare. They were in thick fog. The pinpoint of green, blurred by the fog, was now focused into a hard green light – the starboard navigation light of a steamer bearing down upon them! It passed very close, and Innes saw that it was one of the Channel Island ferries with lit portholes and steaming lights riding high like misted stars.

The two men watched it pass in the fog, wondering why they had not heard the engines, the wind being northerly, thinking how lucky they were that it hadn't run them down. Innes could see the glimmer of the bridge, and suddenly it came to him: suppose it had been a sort of *Mary Celeste*, the lights still burning, the engines running – and nobody at the wheel, nobody on the bridge, nobody in the whole ship.

He went back down to the chart table, switched on the light and entered the incident up in the log. At the end he added, 'What a marvellous opening for a book?' He recalled later that everything that happens to a writer – good or bad – is all grist to the mill.

That was the moment when Innes's novel *The Wreck of the Mary Deare* began to grow in his mind.

# A GHOST OF DIMINISHING RETURNS

## ATLANTIC OCEAN, 1957

The *Pamir* was a sail-training vessel in the German merchant service, commanded by Captain Diebitsch. Under him were 35 crew members and 51 sea cadets, aged 16–18.

The *Pamir* had originated from Hamburg's Blohm and Voss shipyard in 1905 alongside another barque, the *Passat*. These were huge, impressive ships, 270ft (82.3m) long with four masts each and an acre of sail.

In August 1957, the *Pamir* left Buenos Aires with a cargo of 3,790 tons of barley. Hurricane Carrie ferociously struck her on 20 September. On 21 September her final message reported all sails lost and a 45-degree list. She was in danger of sinking.

The US freighter *Saxon* raced to the rescue but only a lifeboat with five survivors was found and one other survivor later. The other 80 seamen had drowned.

The story should have ended there, but it didn't. Mysteriously, the phantom of the *Pamir* has been variously spotted: by the sail-trainer *Esmereld* from Chile during a gale in the English Channel; by a yachtsman off the Virgin Islands; by two other training vessels, one German and another Norwegian. Even the US Coast Guard vessel the *Eagle* reported a sighting. Apparently, each time she was seen, the crew of the *Pamir* lined up on deck – and each time fewer men can be counted. At the last sighting only 20 men materialised.

Whether she is still haunting the seas remains to be seen.

# MORE DEAD THAN ALIVE
## ATLANTIC OCEAN, 1957

When a capsized trimaran was spotted by a passing cargo ship, none of those on board could have imagined that theirs was the third vessel to sail so close to the destitute, shipwrecked sailor clinging to the hulk, by this time more dead than alive.

Wolfgang Kraker von Shwartzenfeld fought for his life when, on 22 July 1957, 1,200 miles (1,931km) east of New York, his boat capsized while he was trying to cross the Atlantic.

He'd spent more than two weeks on top of his upturned boat, constantly wet and cold, feverishly hungry and thirsty. He had fought desperately to survive by fishing and drinking saltwater, had battled with sharks and had endured excruciating pains in his joints and the agonies caused by suppurating sores.

Imagine, then, how bitter his disappointment must have been when, despite all his efforts at survival, he found himself helplessly stranded between two passing ships who had been too busy communicating with each other via Morse lamp to notice his desperate plight!

He now lay in the miniature inflatable dinghy that he'd tied between the main hull and the outrigger and decided to make his peace with himself and the world. Eventually, he had sunk into the blissful oblivion of hallucination, the inevitable prelude to death in such a situation. He had closed his eyes and drifted off to sleep – almost.

Suddenly, his eyelids opened, as if alerted by something, some sixth survival sense. Wolfgang saw a ship!

In spite of his desperate state, he managed to scramble onto the top of the upturned boat, pulling his dinghy with him. He hoisted it above his head. The ship stopped!

He was taken aboard, almost dead. In fact, one of the crew joked with him later that they'd wondered if it might have been better to have thrown him back in!

One week later, however, he stepped ashore in Monrovia, very much alive again.

# THE GHOSTS OF A QUEEN

## ENGLAND, 1966

One of the most famous of all cruise ships, the *Queen Mary* – now a hotel and tourist attraction – is said to be host to several ghosts. One may be the spirit of John Pedder, a 17-year-old crewman who was crushed to death by a watertight door in 1966 during a routine drill. Pedder had lied about his age in order to get the job. Knocking has been heard from the pipes around the door on more than one occasion, once progressing in a circle all the way around a group of tourists. Another time, two people saw a bright light with smoke in front of it as though with a fire. The woman also felt heat from the doorway when she touched it. A tour guide reported that she saw a darkly dressed figure as she was leaving the area where Pedder had been killed. She saw his face and recognised that it was Pedder from his photographs.

Another ghost, dressed in blue-grey overalls and sporting a long beard, has been spotted in the shaft alley of Engine Room 2. Many stowaways died when the ship's boilers were fired up to leave port, and sometimes a feeling of vast despair can be felt on the catwalk and also on the shuffleboard deck above.

Ghostly voices and laughter have been heard by the ship's swimming pool. One employee saw the wet footprints of a child appearing on the pool deck when no one was there, but where on other occasions two different children have been seen, one a girl who asks after her mother or her doll, and a boy. The girl at the pool is also commonly seen around the third-class stairwell, near the door to the old nursery. The girl is thought to have been a precocious child from third class who liked sliding down banisters and was doing so when the ship hit a swell and pitched so that the banister went straight down and she hit the wall, breaking her neck.

A man screams for help, sometimes, or moans in pain. This is thought to have originated during the Second World War, when, during one of its trips to Europe, the *Queen Mary* hit another, much smaller, ship, broadsiding it. The other ship was cut nearly in two by the force while the *Queen Mary* sustained little damage.

When the ship reached port, it was sent to dry dock for repairs to the hull, the outer section of which had been badly torn. When they drained the water, they found the body of a man who had been thrown through a hole torn in the hull above the waterline from the smaller ship and who had died of exposure.

The last story concerns a special cabin. During one crossing, a man checked in at the desk, and his luggage was stowed. That night he asked one of the stewards if he could find a female companion for the night and gave the steward a small wad of bills. The steward found a willing companion and she and the passenger retired for the night. The next morning, when the man didn't come to the dining room for breakfast, the steward knocked at his room.

After receiving no answer, he fetched the head steward, who opened the room. The walls and bed were covered in the blood of the woman, who had been murdered. A check of the registrar revealed that there had been no passenger assigned to the room, and, when they looked for his luggage, there was none to be found, even though many people remember its being checked and stowed.

# DONALD CROWHURST AND THE GOLDEN GLOBE

## ATLANTIC OCEAN, 1969

Of all the entrants to the Golden Globe Round the World Race of 1969, Donald Crowhurst was perhaps the most surprising. His educational background in high-tech electronics was somewhat removed from the world of sailing in 1968 but it was for this reason that he felt he would have an advantage over his fellow competitors, as his boat would be very different.

He devised a clever system to avoid capsizing. Electrodes on the boat's sides would detect submergence and trigger the inflation of a buoyancy bag on the mast. Another novel idea was that sensors in the rigging would detect changes in the weather, adjusting the sails automatically. Unfortunately, because of poor planning and the haste of completion, hardly any of this came to fruition.

Departure was disorganised chaos. Carpenters and painters were working on her until almost the last moment. The signs were there from the beginning that this wasn't to be his race: the champagne bottle failed to smash at the launch of his trimaran, then a burn to the hand erased the lifeline on his palm (sailors are a superstitious lot). After he had finally set off, just hours before the deadline, a box was found on the quay, full of vital repair equipment.

Crowhurst crammed the boat with electronic paraphernalia, intending to build his 'computer' en route. How cruelly ironic that his generator soon became badly damaged by seawater, depriving him of power for much of the time. Even when he had electricity he had to bail by hand, as the suction pipe for the pumps had been mistakenly left on the quayside in Teignmouth. The heavy rubber buoyancy bag hung flaccid from the mast throughout the voyage, unconnected and useless.

It soon became obvious that his hastily prepared craft had no chance of success. Instead of facing the Southern Ocean, he chose the route of deception, remaining in the Atlantic, sending back vague reports and false positions, even stopping for repairs in South America. For months, he zigzagged aimlessly about the Atlantic, lost in self-doubt and his obsession with electronics.

On his homeward run up the Atlantic, another of the Golden Globe competitors, Lieutenant Commander Nigel Tetley, was startled by reports that Crowhurst was close behind him. Pressing hard through a storm near the Azores, Tetley's standard trimaran disintegrated and sank. Now, all attention focused on Crowhurst. It seemed inevitable that he would win the prize for the fastest circumnavigation.

But Crowhurst's impending 'triumph', the loneliness and the strain of his deception became too much to bear. On 10 July 1969, his trimaran yacht *Teignmouth Electron* was spotted drifting in mid-Atlantic by the Royal Mail vessel *Picardy*. No one appeared to be aboard and blasts on the foghorn brought no response. A boarding party reached the vessel, which they found deserted, like the *Mary Celeste*. The life raft was still in place, although conditions inside were squalid with dishes piled in the sink and wires and electrical components scattered everywhere.

There was no sign of Donald Crowhurst, but the vessel had not been hit by bad weather or a freak wave, since a soldering iron was still balanced on a tin of milk. There were also a logbook in which the last entry was 23 June and navigation charts on which positions had been mapped. Also found were 25,000 words of Crowhurst's final diary.

The boat was salvaged and brought back to Britain, together with the diary.

The diary revealed the deterioration of Crowhurst's mind, from small lies that he had begun with his false signals, into a condition that might be described as an insane mystical state.

He wrote of a philosophy and system that controlled humanity, of evolution into a god, of a 'World Brain' and leaving the body. The diary suggested Crowhurst had committed suicide.

When he had failed to make a scheduled radio call, a large-scale search for him was instigated across the entire Atlantic. If a yacht is reported missing, most ships will keep a better lookout in the relevant area. This is even more the case when the missing yachtsman is a well-known single-handed sailor who is apparently nearing the end of a circumnavigation that has lasted several months and is the probable winner of a substantial sum of money. So it is little wonder that, though *Teignmouth Electron* wasn't found immediately, at least four other yachts were found in the area between Bermuda and the Azores within a week.

In the course of the same search the cargo ship *Maple Bank* sighted the white hulls of a 60ft (18.3m) catamaran on 1 July drifting keel-up 300 miles (483km) northeast of Bermuda. No survivors were found.

On the 6 July the cargo ship *Golar Frost* found the small Swedish sailing cruiser *Vaga*, which had sailed under full sail across the Atlantic with no one on board. The captain sent a party across to the boat, who established that it belonged to the Swedish single-handed yachtsman Peter Wallin, whose last log entry was dated 2 July. The boat was in good order, sailing well and completely undamaged. The owner is assumed to have fallen overboard and drowned.

On 4 July, the steamer *Cotopaxi* sighted a 30ft (9.1m) cruising yacht sailing east, apparently unmanned. The ship let the yacht sail past without attempting to board her.

On 8 July the tanker *Helisoma* sighted a capsized yacht, probably a multi-hull, of around 36ft (11m) in length between the Azores and the Portuguese coast. The captain of the tanker reported the drifting yacht as a 'danger to shipping'.

Competitor Nigel Tetley, who had believed Crowhurst's false reports and had believed they were neck and neck in the race, would also eventually kill himself. Awarded a consolation prize of £1,000, he put the money towards a new boat on which he planned another circumnavigation attempt in 1972. But a book he wrote of his experiences failed to sell and he was unable to attract sponsorship to pay for the sails, equipment and food for the voyage. Tetley disappeared in February 1972 and three days later his body was found hanging from a tree in Ewell Minnis Wood, near Dover.

Meanwhile, the *Teignmouth Electron* had been sold first as a tourist boat at Montego Bay and then to Winston Dermott, a Canadian who ran a scuba-diving business on Grand Cayman Island. Both McDermott and a young Jamaican he employed on the boat believed it was haunted. Footsteps were heard pacing the deck. Was this the ghost of Donald Crowhurst?

One night the trimaran was damaged in a hurricane on the island of Cayman Brac. It is still there, lying near the beach in the weeds, sun-bleached and forgotten, with the name the *Teignmouth Electron* still just visible on the prow and stern.

# FOLLOW THAT GIRL!

## SAN FRANCISCO, USA, 1971

It was 20 September 1971 when Leonard Delmas, an experienced sailor, left San Francisco Yacht Club in San Francisco Bay in his boat, *Another Girl*. He intended to sail home to Marin County, east of the Golden Gate Bridge.

On this occasion, he was in a hurry, so he set the sails while motoring at full speed. In the middle of the bay, while he was manipulating the tiller extension, his lifeline broke and he fell backwards into the water. Luckily, the mainsheet was caught around his foot, attaching him to the boat, which now tacked but still motored on at full throttle. He was now being towed along by his own yacht at a speed of 5 knots (9.3km/h).

The water being fairly cold and with no other vessel in sight in the darkness, he now had two options: he could stay with her or try to swim ashore. He decided to keep hold and try to regain control of the boat.

Various efforts to climb back aboard failed, however. All he could do was pull himself up the stern of the boat so he could just reach the toe rail with his outstretched hand. Once, he managed to pull himself up on the mounting bracket of the lifebuoy, but when he got to deck level the fitting broke and he fell back into the water. Time and again he fell back into the water – at one point dangerously near the exhaust outlet. Each time he saved himself.

To his chagrin, he now noticed that the yacht was going

round in circles, but that no one had noticed anything untoward! Two hours passed and he was beginning to feel his physical resources rapidly diminishing. Another hour, and he was almost at the end of his tether – when he realised he was heading for an offshore passenger launch harbour.

Now he felt sure his boat would ram one of the launches, and he had just made up his mind to let go and swim to one of the other boats when suddenly his boat stopped, held by one of the mooring ropes. Thirty minutes later, he had managed to climb onto one of the launches. At last he was on dry deck – but very, very cold and still offshore. He had no choice but to gingerly pull his yacht towards him, climb back on board and return whence he had set off, the St Francis Yacht Club, four long and frustrating hours ago!

Leonard died on 13 November 2015.

# THE PRIME MINISTER'S NOT FOR TURNING

## FASTNET RACE, 1971

In 1971, the late Conservative Prime Minister, Edward Heath, steered the British Admiral's Cup team to victory at the helm of his 42ft (12.8m) yacht, *Morning Cloud*. He sailed into Plymouth at the end of the punishing 605 mile (974km) long Fastnet race to cheers from the crowd after a five-day race that had taken him from Cowes on the Isle of Wight to the Fastnet Rock off the Irish coast and back to Plymouth.

*Morning Cloud* was the last of the three British yachts to return, in fourteenth place overall, but with enough points to secure the return of the Admiral's Cup to Britain. Looking jubilant as he stepped onto dry land, Heath told waiting reporters, 'I am absolutely delighted we won. It has been a team effort throughout.'

During the race, however, Heath – later Sir Edward – had had to weather storms not only in the Atlantic Ocean, but also from critics at home who condemned his decision to stay in the race despite a growing crisis in Northern Ireland. The decision by Northern Ireland's Prime Minister, Brian Faulkner, to impose internment of suspected terrorists without trial was taken while Heath was still at sea, and his Deputy Prime Minister, Reginald Maudling, had to deal with the emergency in his place.

At a news conference shortly after his arrival at Plymouth, Heath refused to discuss Northern Ireland, saying only that he had been kept closely informed of events by radio link.

It was left to his press officer, Henry James, to explain that all decisions on the government's course of action had been taken before Heath had sailed. He said the Prime Minister went on board the *Morning Cloud* as planned to avoid raising the alarm that something unusual was afoot. There were contingency plans in place to lift Heath off the yacht by helicopter, but, if that had happened, *Morning Cloud* would have been disqualified and Britain's chances of winning the Admiral's Cup would have virtually disappeared.

As it was, Britain was 43 points clear of the previous holders of the Admiral's Cup, the United States, in second place, and Australia in third. Edward Heath would win the race four times, three of them in consecutive years in the early 1970s on *Morning Cloud II*, *Morning Cloud III* and in 1980 on *Morning Cloud IV*.

Heath's determination not to be swayed by distracting events was noted by others. John Belcher, a well-known yachtsman, had developed a highly successful technique for distracting the opposition while rounding a buoy in a race. Among his crew were a number of seductive young women, one of whom would entwine herself around him as he manhandled the sails during critical phases of a race.

The crew of nearby yachts rounding a marker would become so fascinated by the spectacle that they would devote more attention to the girl than to their own spinnakers, which would invariably end up wrapped round the forestay. Meanwhile, Belcher's spinnaker would be smartly stowed and he would be beating along the next tack, in the lead.

The only time Belcher's stratagem completely failed was in the Solent during a Point Championships race, when the boat he was trying to distract was *Morning Cloud* (Mark I, the 34ft (10.4m) version). Edward Heath and his staunch crew were above being diverted by this sort of thing, and Belcher became more distracted than they were. A chalice was duly raised to Heath during the celebration dinner, and the toast was, 'To a man of iron will and purpose.'

# *LUCETTE*
# AND THE TURTLE
## GALAPAGOS ISLANDS, 1972

On 15 June 1972, Dougal Robertson, his wife, three children and a young friend were aboard their 39ft (11.9m) schooner, *Lucette*, some 200 miles (322km) from the Galapagos Islands, preparing for the last stretch before landfall on the Marquesas, when there came a sudden, wrenching blow that staggered them all. Had they struck a reef?

Robertson, who was below working at his chart table, immediately knew better – for poking through the deck planking almost at his feet was the head of a killer whale! The *Lucette* had been attacked by a pod of at least four such whales, the one Robertson was staring at having apparently killed itself by smashing its head against the lead keel.

He quickly set up emergency procedures. The 9ft (2.7m) fibreglass dinghy was cut loose plus two rafts, and a three-day survival pack. As the *Lucette* sank within seconds, there was no time to save the sextant and chart, or to take more food and water. The other killer whales, perhaps distracted by the death of their comrade, paid no attention as the family scrambled into the dinghy and rafts and paddled around the scene trying to collect a few items from the flotsam, anything that would help them survive.

Robertson and his family now had to try to survive by relying on raw courage, incredible ingenuity and sheer hope. For 37 days, they struggled to prevent dehydration by giving themselves enemas with brackish water and feeding themselves by catching small fish, dolphins, sharks and turtles with fishhooks from the survival kit. Some of the fish was eaten raw, the rest sun-dried. Moisture was obtained from the eyes of the fish and the blood of a 70-odd pound (31.8kg) turtle!

The turtle arrived when one late afternoon they felt an unusually hard bump on the raft floor. Looking out from the stern door of the raft, they found themselves gazing at the large scaly head of a turtle, protruding eyes set above a nasty-looking beak. They decided to try to catch it.

The turtle's flipper had become entangled in the sea anchor line so, first passing a rope from the dinghy under the raft, they made it fast to one of the back flippers, then, carefully avoiding the searching beak, freed the turtle from the sea anchor rope and towed it around the raft to the dinghy. Robertson then scrambled onto the dinghy and pulled the now struggling turtle alongside, reaching down to grasp the back flippers.

He twisted the turtle round until its back was next to the dinghy and heaved. It was surprisingly heavy as it came aboard, tilting the dinghy alarmingly and forcing Robertson to throw his weight to the other side to trim her. Then, with a bump and a thrashing of claws, the reptile lay on its back in the bottom of the dinghy.

The difficult part was where to cut to reach the artery. Robertson grasped a pointed knife in his right hand and, putting a foot on each of the front flippers, held the turtle's beak with his left hand, then plunged the knife into the leathery skin of the neck, deep into the spinal column. With quick, outward strokes of the knife to right and left he cut both vein and artery. Deep red blood spurted into the bottom of the dinghy and, gradually, beak and flippers ceased thrashing as the beast died.

Robertson washed the blood from his hands into the bottom of the dinghy, careful not to spill any in the water and so attract any inquisitive sharks until they had started moving again, for if the sharks suspected that the blood came from the raft they would attack the inflatable with disastrous consequences.

He later admitted that, 24 hours previously, he wouldn't have had the stomach for such a bloody business but that the laws of survival applied and the first principle, 'The fittest survive, the weakest go to the wall', had now become their way of life.

When finally picked up by the Japanese trawler *Toka Maru*, 700 miles (1,127km) to the north off the coast of Costa Rica, Robertson estimated that they had sufficient supplies for 14 more days.

Dougal went on to write *Sea Survival: A Manual*, and continued to sail until his death in 1992.

# ADRIFT IN A DINGHY FOR 117 DAYS

## OFF GUATEMALA, 1973

In 1968, when Maralyn and Maurice Bailey sold their house and bought a yacht, nothing could have prepared them for the trials and ordeals that lay in store for them.

They set sail from Southampton in June 1972 in their 31ft (9.4m) yacht *Auralyn*. Their intention was to sail to New Zealand and settle there.

All went well, and Maralyn was in constant touch with her mother via postcards until February 1973, when the cards suddenly stopped.

A diary entry for 4 March 1973 recorded the events that would cast them adrift off the coast of Guatemala for 117 days. They sailed past a whaling vessel and shortly after that they felt an enormous impact on the boat. There was a massive shuddering and splintering and tearing of wood. They dashed onto the deck and saw a huge whale swimming very close to them. Then they saw the damage to the boat. A very large hole had been smashed into the hull by the whale.

Water was pouring in – the boat would go down very soon. They inflated their rubber dinghy and tied it to the life raft. After roping the two boats together, they threw in whatever they could grab – tins of food, a small oil burner, a map, sextant and compass, rubber and glue to patch the dinghy, water containers, knives, plastic mugs and passports – and cut themselves adrift. And so their ordeal began.

They proved themselves to be very resourceful, physically and mentally. They concocted games, played dominoes and made various elaborate plans for the future. At this point there was plenty of rainwater and, when their food supplies ran out, they caught birds and fish and even six young sharks.

Failing rescue, they hoped to drift to the Galapagos Islands; but the weeks passed and no land came in sight. Various ships were sighted but, despite their desperate efforts, no one saw them.

Months elapsed and their struggle for survival became dire. They suffered malnutrition, dehydration and acute sunburn. There were ferocious storms and sharks. The dinghy overturned three times and eventually began to deteriorate. It couldn't last much longer.

Then, unbelievably, on 30 June 1973, a Korean fishing boat, the *Weolmi*, spotted them and managed to get them on board. They were saved – just in time – from certain death.

The great kindness with which the Korean crew treated them ensured a slow but complete recovery back to good health. They were taken to Honolulu with plans already in their heads for putting to sea again in another yacht!

When Maralyn died in 2002, her husband paid a moving tribute to her steadfastness and tenacity. She had been the key, he said, to their survival.

# THE BIGGER THEY COME

## GREAT LAKES, USA, 1975

By 2.15p.m. on 9 November 1975, the *Edmund Fitzgerald*, a giant lakes freighter, had filled her cargo hold with 26,116 tons of taconite pellets in Superior, Wisconsin, and was on her way south to Detroit, as an uneventful shipping season ran down. At 729ft (222m) long, she was at that time the largest freighter on the Great Lakes. With a 75ft (22.9m) beam and a depth of 39ft (11.9m), she had a load capacity of almost 30,000 tons, weighed 13,632 tons and cost $8.4 million.

On 8 November 1975, in the Oklahoma panhandle, the beginnings of a storm stirred the air. Picking up force, the storm moved through Iowa and Wisconsin. On 9 November, gale warnings were issued for Lake Superior. There were 29 men aboard on that November day, captained by Ernest McSorley, aged 63, of Toledo.

At 7a.m. Captain McSorley contacted his company to report that weather would delay his arrival at the Soo Locks. The *Arthur M. Anderson*, under the helm of Captain Jessie B. Cooper, was following the *Fitzgerald* at a distance of nearly 16 miles (25.7km) and keeping in contact. Winds were high, and getting worse. Waves were 8–10ft (2.4–3m) in the early afternoon and increasing in power and size as the day wore on. As heavy snow began to fall, visibility became nil and the *Edmund Fitzgerald* disappeared from the *Arthur M. Anderson*'s view. Waves reached 12–16ft (3.7–4.9m), whipped by winds gusting up to 90mph (145km/h) at the Soo Locks, which were shut down. The Coast Guard issued an emergency warning: all ships were to find safe harbour. By 6p.m. the crashing waves were 25ft (7.6m) high.

McSorley's radar went out, so he slowed his ship to allow the *Arthur M. Anderson* to catch up and guide him.

At 7.10p.m. the *Arthur M. Anderson* radioed the *Fitzgerald* to warn of another vessel 9 miles (14.5km) ahead, but they assured McSorley that on present course the ship would pass by to the west. The first mate of the *Arthur M. Anderson* signed off by asking, 'How are you making out with your problem?' The *Fitzgerald* replied, 'We are holding our own.' It was the last contact with the ship.

The snow was letting up and the *Arthur M. Anderson*'s crew began sighting other ships. None was the *Fitzgerald*. The 729ft (222m) mammoth was missing. A search was launched. Aircraft and patrol boats criss-crossed the area.

Eventually, the *Arthur M. Anderson* discovered a piece of a lifeboat. A life preserver was found. Another lifeboat, a raft, a stepladder; but no bodies, hardly any trace of the huge ore carrier. The search continued for three days.

On 14 November, a navy plane located the wreck. It was just 17 miles (27.4km) from its safe harbour destination of Whitefish Point, 530ft (161m) down on the bottom of Lake Superior. The vessel was in two huge sections on the lake's floor, the metal torn and twisted from the force of the impact.

There was never a definitive account concerning the cause of the *Fitzgerald* wreck. A Coast Guard report suggesting that the hatches had not been closed properly was rejected. Popular speculation held that, as it passed so close to the Caribou Island shoal, the extra 3ft (0.9m) of depth load allowed the hull to scrape the shoals, whose depth was misreported on navigational charts at the time. Some believe that the towering waves caused the steamer to break in two.

Human error, poor maintenance, huge waves – all have been put forward as the reason why this giant ship simply broke in two. None can now be proved.

# THE TRIPLE CLANGER
## ISLE OF WIGHT, ENGLAND, 1978

Among the multitude of small boats bobbing about on the waters of the Solent hoping to see some of the sailing at Cowes, Isle of Wight, in 1978 was a 22ft (6.7m) fibreglass 'weekender' called *Seal*. This particular *Seal*, riding rather low in the water with 11 people on board, was the prototype of the class designed by Angus Primrose, who was there that day with his wife, children, friends Polly Drysdale and Angela Kirby, various young men in high spirits and pretty girls in bikinis. It was warm and sunny, so the party set off for lunch and a swim in Osborne Bay.

Before they had got very far out of Cowes, glasses were filled and a general sense of bonhomie prevailed. So many sails of every size and shape were visible and so many craft were crossing each other's tracks that they were not surprised to be hailed by two young men in a Flying Fifteen who seemed to be in trouble.

They had broken their rudder, one of the young men explained. Could *Seal* possibly give them a tow back to their mooring? This was, of course, the last thing anyone wanted to do on such a nice day, with a party under way and the prospect of lunch and a swim close at hand. Primrose replied in tones of hearty rebuke, 'Sorry, old chap, but when I was your age I learned how to sail myself home without a rudder. If you don't learn now you never will. There's no way I'm going to turn back at this stage and waste everyone's morning towing back every Tom, Dick and Harry who gets into trouble.'

On they sailed. Finally, amid much jollity, they reached their destination and dropped anchor, and, by the time most of the party had had a dip and preparations were in hand for lunch, it was well into the afternoon. Suddenly, Primrose noticed a familiar boat anchored not far away: Admiral Morrice McMullen's 32ft (9.7m) wooden yacht *Fidget*.

In contrast to the fairly orgiastic scene now visible on *Seal*, everything aboard *Fidget* looked quiet and sedate. A group of well-dressed people were on board drinking tea. Feeling that it was rather boring of them to be drinking tea so early in the afternoon – it was barely four o'clock – Primrose cried out cheerily, 'Ahoy there, Morrice, what are you doing with that dreary-looking crowd? Why not come over and join us and have some fun?'

The admiral's reply was diplomatically noncommittal – even a trifle chilling.

Eventually, everyone decided to get a bit nearer the action. 'Let's go and have a look at *Britannia*,' someone said, and off they went. As the royal yacht's massive hull loomed closer there was a sudden change in wind direction. Primrose, his nose in a gin and tonic at this point, realised that action was called for. 'Lee-ho!' he shouted. Polly Drysdale, at the helm, slammed the tiller over hard and collided with *Britannia* just aft of the companionway.

'We thought you might be the party coming aboard for tea,' joked a rating as he helped push them off with a boathook.

'No, I'm afraid we'll never get invited if we carry on like that,' replied Primrose.

There was some conflict of opinion about what happened after that. Was there a second collision – or perhaps a near-miss – with HMS *Leopard*, the destroyer on guard? Several present do remember being rather too close to a surface-to-air missile for comfort, and everyone agrees that a concoction known as 'Shangri-la' (like Sangria but with brandy and curaçao added) was produced. And drunk. Several observers at one point called out encouragingly to the woman at *Seal*'s helm: 'Carry on, Polly, we think you're doing *awfully* well!'

That evening at Dot's bar, one of the first bits of news Primrose heard was that Prince Andrew had lost his rudder in the Flying Fifteen race and someone had refused him a tow. Then a voice said, 'Did you see Morrice McMullen had Princess Alexandra and her children on board *Fidget* for tea?'

The following day, as everyone crowded into the tent of the boat-builder Groves and Gutteridge in the pouring rain, news of the triple clangers quickly spread and was just as quickly dubbed 'Primrose's hat trick'.

'Well done, skipper,' remarked the cartoonist Andrew Spedding, clapping Primrose on the back. 'You won't get the OBE this year!'

# FASTNET DISASTER

## ATLANTIC OCEAN, 1979

The Fastnet Race was the last in a series of five that made up the Admiral's Cup competition, the world championship of yacht racing.

The first Fastnet Race, on 15 August 1925, attracted seven boats to the start line. The fleet consisted mainly of a collection of old cruising boats starting the race from the Royal Victorian Yacht Club at Ryde. It turned out to be a typical race for the course, with the faster yachts making good time and safely in port, while the slower entries were hit by high winds and uncomfortable seas. Two boats retired and one made such slow progress that she was unable to reach the finishing line before the timekeepers had gone home. The race quickly evolved due to the popularity of the new sport of ocean racing in England.

It was not until 1957 however that the Admiral's Cup was introduced. As a private challenge by five well-known British yachtsmen to their American counterparts, it consisted of a series of races that included the Fastnet as the last one.

The Admiral's Cup soon became known as the most hotly contested ocean racing event in the world and the Fastnet as one of the toughest ocean racing challenges. The 1927, 1930, 1949 and 1957 races went down on record as being the toughest Fastnets ever. In 1957 there were 29 retirements from the fleet of 41 yachts. Two years later the Admiral's Cup was thrown open to teams from all nations.

By the 1970s British ocean racing saw a great upsurge in popularity with heroes such as Francis Chichester, Robin Knox-Johnston and the then leader of the Conservative Party, Edward Heath, achieving seventh in class with *Morning Cloud* in the 1969 Fastnet and going on to lead the British Admiral's Cup team to victory in 1971 (see 'The Prime Minister's Not For Turning', page 193).

On Saturday, 11 August 1979, the field of 303 set off from Cowes on a sunny day with a pleasant breeze behind them. The course took them westwards, across the Irish Sea, around Fastnet Rock off the coast of the Republic of Ireland and back to Plymouth.

By the Monday lunchtime force seven winds were on their way but the field, who included Edward Heath, were confident of weathering the storm. However, the forecasters had underestimated the strength of the winds, which buffeted the competitors throughout that day and whipped up mountainous waves.

Walls of water 40ft (12.2m) high crashed down on the field and tricky tides exacerbated the situation. A string of mayday calls were sent out and British and Irish naval vessels, lifeboats and even a Dutch frigate came to the rescue of the stricken sailors. A total of 114 seamen were rescued by ships and helicopters but 23 yachts had to be abandoned to the cruel sea.

The crew of the *Ariadne*, who had been battered by huge waves for several hours, were too tired to climb a ladder dangling from a rescue helicopter. Four of the ship's six-strong crew died. There were also casualties on the yachts *Grimalkin*, *Trophy*, *Festina Tertia*, *Flashlight* and *Veronier II*. Six lives were lost because their safety harnesses broke, and another nine people drowned or died of hypothermia in their yachts or life rafts.

Afterwards the Royal Ocean Racing Club was heavily criticised, but its secretary, Allan Green, said attempts to abandon the race had been frustrated by the lack of proper radio equipment on about half of the competing boats. 'Sailors must make up their own minds whether to face the risks of the sea or not.'

A Fastnet Memorial now stands in the gardens of the Holy Trinity Church, Cowes – a rock sculpture erected in memory of the sailors who tragically lost their lives in the Fastnet race of 1979.

Normally a biennial event (occurring in odd-numbered years) the event was not staged in 2001 and was last held in 2003. It was cancelled at short notice in 2005.

# NATALIE WOOD'S (NOT SO) SPLENDID DEATH

## CALIFORNIA, USA, 1981

Labelled the 'brunette bombshell', Natalie Wood was one of the few performers able to make the transition from successful child star to successful adult actress.

Her role in *Rebel Without a Cause* earned her an Oscar nomination for Best Supporting Actress and she went on to play many diverse roles and dated some of Hollywood's most eligible men.

In 1957, she married Robert Wagner, only to divorce him in 1963. They remained cordial when they met socially and, two divorces later, they were remarried on 16 June 1972 on their yacht *Splendour*, named after her 1961 movie *Splendour in the Grass*, in which she co-starred with former love Warren Beatty. On the afternoon of 29 November 1981, off the Catalina Coast, Wood, Wagner and the actor Christopher Walken were aboard the *Splendour*. Wood and Walken awoke from naps before Wagner, and the pair went ashore in the dinghy and drank for a couple of hours in a Catalina restaurant. Wagner later joined them for more drinks and a dinner with wine. All were quite drunk when they returned to the *Splendour* at 10p.m. Wood was aware that she was at a crossroads in her career and was taking steps to transform and revitalise it. She was to star in her first play, *Anastasia*, and had optioned as a producer and potential star the rights to the biography of Zelda Fitzgerald. She also had aspirations to direct. During the extensive drinking bout that evening, however, Wagner complained that his wife spent too much time on her acting career at the expense of their children. Against his better judgement, Walken sided with Wood, advising her husband to let her do what she wanted to do. They argued into the night. Wood and Walken retired to their staterooms and Wagner remained topside with the pilot. Sometime later, Wagner went to the master stateroom to check on Wood and found she wasn't there. The dinghy, which had been tied beside the boat, was also missing.

Walken notified the authorities and a search began. The dinghy was soon discovered in a Catalina cove. Shortly before dawn, the body of the 43-year-old actress was found floating face down in open sea; her parka had kept her afloat.

The Los Angeles County Coroner's Office decided that Wood had died accidentally, 'possibly attempting to board the dinghy and had fallen into the water, striking her face'. The rumours, however, now started: was it murder?

Robert Wagner issued one public statement through his attorney in 1981, speculating that Wood had left the boat to take the dinghy ashore. Later that same year, a friend of his issued a second statement offering a different theory: that Wood slipped and fell off the boat while attempting to retie the dinghy, which he thought might have been keeping her awake by bumping against the side of the boat.

Both explanations are problematic. Natalie Wood had never been known to take the dinghy alone at night. As for the second theory, the coroner's investigator, Paul Miller, examined the yacht and the dinghy and said that Wood would not have been able to hear a bumping dinghy from her stateroom.

The question that perplexed most people was why the three men on the boat waited at least an hour and a half from the time they told police they had first noticed her missing before looking for her or calling for help.

It would also have been odd for Wood to be alone on a

dinghy at night in any attire, since she suffered from hydrophobia (fear of water). In fact, the night before she drowned, she had baulked at getting into the dinghy even with her husband and Chris Walken aboard. Because of the amount of drink consumed that day and that night, the details may be lost in an alcoholic haze.

Sadly, despite three Oscar nominations, Wood is now most often remembered for her death by drowning off Catalina Island.

# ORDEAL BY RAFT

## MAINE, USA, 1982

In 1982, aged 24 and with a Whitbread Round the World regatta under her belt, sailor Debbie Kiley boarded a 58ft (17.7m) sailing yacht in Maine for a routine delivery to Florida.

There were five crew members: the skipper John Lippoth, his girlfriend Meg Mooney, Mark Adams, Brad Cavanaugh and Debbie Kiley. Brad and Mark were very competent sailors, although Mark was considered a bit of a wild man and a drinker. John had done a lot of sailing, but was also a big drinker, and his girlfriend was only a fair-weather sailor.

When they left the harbour the weather report was clear, but after the second day the weather began to deteriorate and by the evening of the second day there were 35ft (10.7m) seas with winds gusting to 60 knots (111km/h). Eventually, the seas were up to 45ft (13.7m) and the winds were a sustained 70 knots (130km/h), gusting to 90 (167km/h).

For close on 11 hours, John, Mark and Meg remained below, drinking, while Brad and Debbie remained on watch. When the drinkers were finally sober enough to stand their watch, Meg came up only to be immediately thrown across the cockpit, hurting her back badly. John called the Coast Guard, who said they were going to send two vessels out to help.

John and Mark took the watch. The next thing Debbie remembered was Brad dragging her out of her berth, shouting, 'C'mon. We're going. We've got to go *now*!' Thinking the Coast Guard had arrived, she jumped out of her bunk only to be hit by knee-high rising water.

As she swam through the main salon of the boat, she noticed water cascading down from the window onto Mark, who was lying on a settee. As it turned out, Mark and John had lashed the steering wheel, gone below and gone back to sleep. Debbie got up on deck to see nothing but huge, tumultuous seas – and no ship in sight.

Mark untied the life raft, but it immediately blew away. They had an inflatable Zodiac boat on deck, and Brad managed to untie it, but, when it popped off the last cleat, the rope sliced into his arm.

They all managed to make it to the Zodiac, but Meg got caught in the rigging on her way there and suffered horrible lacerations – almost to the bone – on her legs and her body. As the yacht sank, they tried to overturn the Zodiac and get into it, but every time they did a wave would blow it back over, scattering them.

For 18 hours they trod water. By the next morning, the weather had slightly improved, and they finally righted the Zodiac. John got in first, then Meg was lifted in. Brad then got in, followed by Mark and Debbie, who looked under the water – to see sharks approaching! Once the group were in the Zodiac, sharks surfaced around them. From that moment on, they stayed.

By the third day, Meg was dying of blood poisoning. Delusions were setting in because of dehydration and hypothermia. On the night of the third day, Mark and John drank saltwater, so by the fourth day they were delirious. John then jumped into the water and swam out a few yards. They heard a loud scream and he disappeared.

By this time Meg had red streaks running up past her groin and was almost catatonic. Mark grew angry and said he was going to go over the side to warm up. Just as he went into the water, Brad caught a small fish; the others were engrossed in trying to eat it when Mark disappeared. They felt a thud against the Zodiac, there was a frenzy under the boat and the sharks tore Mark to pieces.

Meg died on the fourth night. Debbie and Brad then passed out and the next thing Debbie knew was that the sun had risen, and Meg's body was in rigor mortis, awash on the bottom of the boat. They buried her at sea.

The remaining two then turned the boat over and washed out the rotten seaweed, urine and the pus from Meg's wounds. Just then Brad said, 'Look. There's a ship.' Debbie's first thought was not to get excited, as they had seen ships before. But this time it was apparent that the ship had seen them.

The swells, however, were huge. The freighter made two passes, and finally, when they got close enough, they threw out two long lines. Debbie jumped overboard but missed one. They then threw a life ring with another line, which Brad grabbed before grasping Debbie.

It wasn't easy climbing up to safety – every time they got close, they would get sucked under the huge freighter and the barnacles would take the skin off their bodies. Finally, they managed to get on board the ship, which dropped them off with the Coast Guard.

Debbie later admitted feeling plagued with guilt. Ultimately, she came to realise that only her sailing experience and deep faith had helped her survive. She felt the Lord's Prayer had had a lot to do with her survival. 'I was letting the big guy know I was not going to give up,' she said.

She went on to write a popular account of the incident called *Albatross: The True Story of a Woman's Survival at Sea* (1994) which was made into a TV film, *Two Came Back*. She became a motivational speaker and published another book in 2006 about lessons for surviving.

Deborah Kiley died on 13 August 2012 in San Miguel de Allende, Mexico.

# DENNIS WILSON'S BAD VIBRATIONS

## CALIFORNIA, USA, 1983

One of the Beach Boys' founder members, Dennis Wilson, owned a 62ft (18.9m) yacht called *Harmony*. He'd bought it when the Beach Boys were at the height of their popularity. It was his pride and joy. He once stood on the boat and looked out into the water and said that the ocean was where he belonged, and that was where he wanted to be buried.

His passion for alcohol and cocaine, however, led to a tortured relationship with the rest of the group. He would be invited back to perform with them, only to relapse and get the sack. He'd go in to rehab and rejoin the group, relapse and leave again. The money became less regular, and he fell behind in his payments on the yacht.

Finally, the bank repossessed it, and Dennis hit rock bottom. His fellow group members cut him off financially, in the hope that he would complete a rehab programme, but Dennis would consistently relapse. He was a generous man who knew how to help everyone except himself.

At the end of December 1983, 39-year-old Dennis was out of rehab, again unsuccessfully. He took to hanging out at the docks where his old yacht used to be berthed. There he met up with his old pal Bill Oster, who had a yacht called *Emerald* near where Dennis had kept *Harmony*.

Oster had been Dennis's neighbour at the Marina during better times and, on that 27 December afternoon, the two men had a reunion of sorts. As guests of Oster, Dennis and Crystal McGovern, his current girlfriend, spent the afternoon and evening enjoying the lifestyle that Dennis had once indulged in. Aboard Oster's yacht, they talked late into the night.

The next morning, with the fresh sea air filling his lungs, Dennis bounded about the *Emerald* like a little boy in a tree house. His first job was to mix himself a screwdriver. Then he and Bill Oster had a great time roaming around the marina in a tiny rowing boat, surprising old friends. That gregarious Beach Boy was back.

Back on board the *Emerald*, everyone had lunch before Dennis astonished his companions by announcing that he was going for a swim. The water was a chilly 58°F (14.4°C) – it was 28 December, after all – and Dennis was pronounced crazy. With a laugh, he dived in, dressed only in cut-off jeans, and began to swim around the dock. He'd been in and out of the water a few times when the idea struck him to dive down beneath where the *Harmony* had once been docked.

There he discovered remnants of his past life, still resting on the marina floor. He surfaced, brandishing a picture that had been thrown from his boat in a moment of anger years earlier. The seven-year-old photograph was of Dennis and his ex-wife Karen during their happiest days, preserved within the sterling-silver frame that a friend had given them as a wedding gift. Dennis wiped the mud from the frame and placed it on the dock. Again, he went down – but never resurfaced.

At 4.40p.m., Oster flagged down a passing harbour patrol boat. After they arrived, it took four divers 45 minutes, working in the dark with a pole, probing the ocean floor, to find Wilson's body in 13ft (4m) of water.

On 4 January 1984, Dennis's family, including several of his children and his brother Carl, were part of a three-boat procession, when Dennis was finally put to rest at sea.

# SAVED BY DOLPHINS

## MEDITERRANEAN, 1985

It was a perfect day for sailing in the Mediterranean when Egon Purkl set out single-handed in his 20ft (6.1m) cruiser, *Skarabaus*. He was 30 miles (48.3km) northwest of the Italian island of Stromboli, the weather was warm and the sea calm, and he was wearing light summer clothing – with no life jacket. The yacht was steering herself and all was right with the world – until he accidentally fell overboard.

He'd attached no lifeline and, to his horror, the boat gradually drifted away. After a vain attempt to catch her, he gave up. He was stranded, totally alone in the sea, 30 miles (48.3km) from dry land.

He then had a stroke of luck – his first of several. He was able to seize upon two floating plastic buoys attached to a piece of old fishing net which afforded him some extra buoyancy. The Mediterranean having a higher salinity than an ocean, it was thus easier for him to stay afloat. The water temperature was 79°F (26.1°C), so he could hope to stay alive for 20 hours or so before he died of hypothermia.

At one point during his ordeal, he saw a ship 2 miles (3.2km) in the distance, which of course could not see him. At this point a number of curious dolphins appeared and circled him. After a while, they left and he swam through the night, suffering badly from the cold and trying to conserve heat and energy.

The next day another, larger, school of dolphins joined

him, playing and diving in and around him, as if taunting him. He was too weary to feel afraid – but suddenly he saw another ship.

Miraculously, it changed its course towards him and he was eventually picked up.

How, he wondered, as he was hauled gratefully aboard, had they spotted him from so far off? One of the crewmen waved his binoculars. He'd been watching the dolphins and had been surprised to see Purkl's head bobbing in the water among them. Purkl had been in the water for 24 hours – it was a miracle he'd survived. It's certain that without the playful dolphins, he would have died a miserable death. Instead, after first aid on the ship and a few days in hospital, he embarked on a search for his boat, which had been salvaged intact by an Italian yachtsman.

# SIMON LE BON – JUST A WATER BABY

## ENGLISH CHANNEL, 1985

During the 605 mile (974km) Fastnet yacht race in August 1985, mountainous seas and high winds left a trail of destruction, forcing half the fleet to quit. In the most dramatic incident, the British pop star Simon le Bon's 77ft (23.5m) *Drum of England*, a $1.6 million racer, overturned 3 miles (4.8km) off the southern English port of Falmouth after its keel sheered off, apparently because it struck rocks.

*Drum* had been tacking along, around 9½ knots (17.6km/h), and had just passed the most beautiful part of the Cornish coast, the Manacles. Le Bon – of Duran Duran fame – had just come off a four-hour watch working the main sheet – bringing it in, letting it out – and moving the traveller. He'd gone below deck and was just falling asleep when the boat turned over.

He later recalled to a journalist that his fellow sailor Rick, who had been asleep above him, fell out of his bunk, 'and I thought, Oh, there's Rick. Why is he lying there? Then I was thrown out of the bunk. I heard a couple of bangs, and then the boat went over sideways. The bastard went over sideways! I couldn't believe it!'

The two men moved quickly towards the hatch but, just at that moment, two heavy sails – which take six men to lift – fell on them. They humped and shunted their way along underneath on their knees. They had just started crawling upwards when they realised the boat had turned turtle.

Extremely frightened by now, they lifted a mainsail off Pascal, a French sailor who was shouting, 'I'm drowning.' But there was little panic. If anybody panicked, he'd probably not survive. 'You subconsciously know that panicking will make you do stupid things, and that's the way you are going to die. There was no place for panic,' Le Bon concluded. They also realised it would be much safer staying inside the hull and not trying to get out. Three minutes after the boat had gone down, an automatic radio beacon, activated by the seawater, had started. While they waited for help, they found life jackets and tried to kick out as many alerts as they could to the people up top.

The frogman who came to pull them out at first scared Le Bon, who felt that, with the goggles, he didn't look like a human being – until he spoke with a Manchester accent!

He had brought Le Bon a life jacket with a breathing tube on it, and said, 'You can breathe through this.' But it increased his buoyancy so that he couldn't get down. He had to let go of the life jacket but couldn't – when the others saw what was happening, they pulled it out of his hand, so that he had to take one deep breath of air.

Le Bon then found it was difficult getting through the ropes and the lifeline around the boat: rigging was hanging down from the deck, and lines were trailing, 'just like a big Portuguese man-of-war jellyfish. That's what it looked like. The wires and ropes were like trying to fight through spaghetti. The diver pulled me down, and I pushed off from the deck. When I came out, I was on my back and the water was totally up my nose. On reaching land, the first thing I did was tread in a cow pat, a big brown pancake. And do you know what? It made me so happy. It was warm. It squashed up through my toes!'

What had caused the mishap was a mystery. The boat's designer, New Zealander Ron Holland, called the accident 'a freak', but the crew's captain, American Skip Novak, a respected racing veteran, hinted that the accident might have been caused by a structural flaw. 'You should be able to drive the boat to hell and back and not have the keel fall off,' he declared.

In all the chaos Le Bon missed a call from Boy George, but Duran Duran's Nick Rhodes got through from a recording studio in New York. 'Hi, nice to know you're still alive, Simon,' he told Le Bon. 'When are you going to come back and finish the mixing?'

# HITLER'S YACHT

## MIAMI, USA, 1989

Hitler is supposed to have ordered the yacht *Ostwind* in 1936, for close on $250,000. It was completed in 1939, one of two yachts built by the Nazi government, each cabin finished in a different fine wood, its sail, over 40ft (12.2m) long, made of a rare Egyptian linen. Its designer was Heinrich Gruber – the most lauded naval architect of the time – and its purpose was to demonstrate the superiority of the Aryan race after a poor German showing in the 1936 Olympic races.

There were always rumours about the yacht, one that Hitler and his mistress Eva Braun used the *Ostwind* for pleasure cruises, another that Hitler had an extraordinary affection for the boat, that it was very important to him, and that, when he talked about it, he always referred to it as his 'special lady'.

Some insisted that Hitler's ghost haunted the decks, that the boat was used as a brothel by high-ranking Nazi officials. Others maintained that the yacht itself was cursed – that it would kill, maim or financially ruin anyone unfortunate enough to own it. It certainly seemed to resist its own destruction.

The *Ostwind* actually spent most of its life in America as war booty transported there by the US Navy in 1947. In 1989, however, a plan was hatched to sink the battered wreck in 250ft (76.2m) of water off Miami Beach to help create an artificial reef. There, it would join more than 50 other vessels that had already been towed out and blown up.

At the correct depth and with sufficient sunlight, the hulks would be rapidly colonised and covered by corals, sponges, sea anemones and marine worms. They, in turn, would provide an abundant food supply and excellent protective cover for many other marine organisms such as crabs, lobsters, shrimp, brittle stars and all types of juvenile and smaller fish.

Miami Beach Commissioner Abe Resnick, a Holocaust survivor from Lithuania, raised more than $20,000 to take the *Ostwind* to Miami Beach, declaring that he wanted to turn a symbol of evil into a symbol of life. He had planned the yacht-sinking to coincide with a cruise marking the fiftieth anniversary of the 'Voyage of the Damned', in which more than 900 Jewish refugees aboard the SS *St Louis* were forced off the Florida coast and back to Europe, where many were killed in concentration camps.

On 4 June, more than 300 people were jammed aboard the tiny *Florida Princess* cruise ship, rocking in 4ft (1.2m) seas, when somehow signals got crossed and the yacht went down too soon. Resnick was at the bow of the *Florida Princess* helping survivors of the *St Louis* toss carnations into the water in memory of Nazi victims, when a sledgehammer prematurely sent the yacht into the sea.

'It was truly an incredible, incredible historic event and suddenly – boom! – somebody made a mistake,' Resnick told the *Palm Beach Post*. Resnick had intended to swing the sledgehammer himself in front of a crowd that included 60 journalists from around the world. 'Hitler's soul is still somewhere there,' he said, before adding, 'I'm just kidding.'

In fact, the wooden yacht had been dropped only 20ft (6.1m) onto a living reef that it was now destroying, in a shipping lane where it presented a hazard to navigation.

Fortunately, a local hotel, the Fontainebleau, paid for the yacht to be raised and resunk in 200ft (61m) of water.

'The really sad thing,' said Ben Mostkoff of the Dade County Environmental Resource Management Department, 'was that in the two weeks that the yacht was in the shallow water, divers had defaced the wreck with anti-Semitic graffiti ...'

By contrast, the *Ostwind*'s sister vessel – the *Nordwind*, a boat with an identical pedigree: built at the same time, by the same people for the same purpose – has never been known as Hitler's yacht. Bought by Lord Hugh Astor who raced her for many years in the Solent and on the North Sea, in the late 1970s Dutch naval architect Gerard Dijkstra turned *Nordwind* into one of the earliest classic yacht restoration projects. She has since participated in many classic races, has rounded Cape Horn and extensively travelled the Strait of Magellan, the Beagle Channel and along the south coast of Chile.

# BACK FROM THE DEAD
## NEW ZEALAND, 1989

John Glennie, owner of the multi-hull *Rose-Noelle*, planned to sail through the Pacific Islands to Tonga, some 745 miles (1,199km) northeast of the Marlborough Sounds, in New Zealand. None of his crew of three – Phil Hoffman, Rick Hellreigel and Jim Nalepka – had much experience. Rick had only recently recovered from brain cancer.

They set sail for Tonga and at first the weather was beautiful and spirits were high. But on the third day they began to feel the force of a storm brewing 100 miles (161km) to the south. Forty-knot (74.1km/h) winds coiled and whipped the swelling seas into a frenzy.

Phil wanted John to get on the radio and phone for a helicopter, but he refused. As the storm mounted, however, and under increasing pressure from his crew, he employed a sea anchor to help stabilise the boat. Unfortunately, it failed. The boat lay broadside and vulnerable to the oncoming waves and barely endured the storm. Finally, in the early hours of 4 June, the wind subsided, but tranquillity after a storm in the South Pacific usually means an encounter with freak waves that essentially come out of nowhere. And this is what happened to the *Rose-Noelle*.

Freezing water came in so quickly through the hatch that, within a matter of minutes, it reached their chests – and then miraculously stopped. The *Rose-Noelle* stabilised, a half-submerged coffin in an icy sea. Startled by the sudden change of events, the men scrambled for safety in the cold dark abyss and huddled together seeking cover in the boat's only remaining dry area, the now-upside-down cabin. For the rest of their voyage the tiny platform would be known as 'the cave'.

They were in dire straits. They had capsized in a remote area below the fortieth parallel, a storm-tossed region known as the Roaring Forties. The upturned vessel was now drifting hopelessly towards South America, 6,000 miles (9,656km) away. No boats go down there; no planes go down there.

Before departing, Glennie had agreed to relay his position to a fellow mariner. But Glennie never radioed his friend. Twenty-six days later, New Zealand search and rescue were searching 600 miles (966km) off her true location! After covering nearly 20,000 sq. miles (51,800 sq. km) of sea, the unproductive search was called off.

As they drifted across the Pacific, water was rationed to three ounces a day, and food was limited to small mouthfuls of rice. Hungry, thirsty and confined together at close quarters, the men were aware that tension between them was rising. Anger was felt towards John, whom the men held responsible for their plight. Thirst consumed their every thought. Severely dehydrated, they believed that nothing short of a miracle could save them. Then, 40 days after the capsize, came a wondrous sight. Rain.

Using makeshift materials, the crew fashioned a water-gathering system of PVC pipes and a bucket on the hull. Soon they had a bucket full of fresh water. With a renewed sense of hope they now focused on food, as their meagre supply had dwindled to almost nothing. Seven weeks after the capsize, they caught their first meal, a groper, weighing about 12–14lb (5.4–6.4kg).

After nearly two months of dissention, they now found themselves unified in the quest for survival. Fishing became a full-time passion, a much-needed distraction from their otherwise dreary existence. Back in New Zealand, the men had been declared dead and they had grappled with the stark realisation that they might never see home again.

But, after three agonising months lost at sea, the crew experienced an incredible reversal of fortune. They saw a boat and planes go by – and ships. Within days, Phil saw a New Zealand seabird, and Rick thought he saw a lighthouse. The next morning land was sighted and John Glennie recognised the familiar outline of New Zealand's Great Barrier Island.

The realisation stunned the crew. Some days later, the *Rose-Noelle* went aground on the reef. As the four men struggled towards land, waves battered what was left of their boat. Too weak to climb very far, the men rested for the night and at daybreak they broke into an empty house to find food. The following day Phil set out to find a phone and contacted a policeman, who thought they were dead.

They did indeed appear to have returned from the dead. The men had endured the longest known period in cold water: 119 days in the sea!

The big question on everyone's lips was – how did the *Rose-Noelle* make it back to New Zealand, when she was headed towards South America? Apparently, she had drifted initially to the northeast, with prevailing westerlies, typical of that part of the southern ocean, and especially for that time of year. But, as it clawed to the north, the upturned boat picked up prevailing southeasterlies and easterlies, on the leading edge of stronger-than-usual high-pressure cells. These delivered the boat and crew to safety. If they had capsized one year earlier, their remains might still be drifting around the high latitudes of the Southern Ocean.

As if to dispel the sceptics, three weeks after the event, cruising friends of John Glennie dropped a message in a bottle over the side of their yacht in the vicinity of the *Rose-Noelle*'s capsize. They were also on their way to Tonga but had delayed their departure because of poor weather.

Both the bottle and the *Rose-Noelle* washed ashore within nine days of each other, and only 50 miles (80.5km) apart.

None of the four men kept in touch, even after an event that would seem to have inextricably bound them together. Apart from Hellreigel and Nalepka, the four men were strangers with little in common.

Twenty-six years later, the three remaining men – Hellreigel died of a brain tumour two years after coming ashore – are still estranged.

# MAXWELL:
# THE MOSSAD CONNECTION
## CANARY ISLANDS, 1991

Robert Maxwell was born into poverty in Czechoslovakia and was decorated for his bravery in the Second World War before going on to establish a vast media and publishing empire. A Labour MP in the 1960s, the socialist millionaire counted many world leaders among his friends and associates, including those of the Eastern bloc.

In November 1991, he was taking a break after a bruising round of allegations about links with the Israeli intelligence service, Mossad, and speculation over the health of his business empire.

His yacht, the *Lady Ghislaine*, named after his daughter, left Santa Cruz in the north of the Canaries at 10p.m. on Monday, 4 November, and put into Puerto de los Cristianos, Tenerife, at 9a.m. on 5 November. An air-and-sea search was launched after the captain of the 180ft (55m) *Lady Ghislaine* notified the Spanish authorities that the 68-year-old chairman of Maxwell Communication Corporation and Mirror Group Newspapers had disappeared.

Maxwell's body was found by a fishing boat floating about 20 miles (32.2km) from Gando on the other side of the neighbouring island of Gran Canaria – more than a hundred miles from the obvious route between the points of departure and arrival. Asked to explain how the body could have got there, Tenerife's civil governor, Angel Delgado, replied, 'That's a good question.'

The body was winched from the Atlantic by a Spanish helicopter. Spanish national radio said he was unclothed and showed no sign of violence.

According to the crew, Maxwell had last been seen at 4.25a.m. the previous day. 'His absence was noted when the boat arrived at los Cristianos at 9a.m.,' the governor added. According to other versions, Maxwell was found to be missing at around 11a.m., when he failed to answer a telephone call to his cabin. Licinio Alonso, director of the Maritime Safety Centre at the Spanish transport ministry, said the alarm was not raised until 1p.m. by a satellite telex via Norway.

A Maxwell company spokesman said, 'His last conversation that I can find was with his son Ian, who spoke to him at 11 o'clock last night when they had a normal business and family conversation and he was in a perfectly good mood.'

Richard Stott, then editor of the *Daily Mirror*, said, 'He went out to the boat at the weekend because he had a cold. I spoke to him last night and he seemed OK.'

A judge ruled out foul play but did not rule on whether Maxwell's death was accidental or a suicide. Investigators discovered that Maxwell's businesses were on the brink of financial collapse, adding to speculation that he may have committed suicide.

Mirror Group's editorial director, Charles Wilson, said he could not imagine any situation that would cause Maxwell to take his own life since, 'he had too much of the arrogance of his own ability to conceive of such a thing'.

In February 1996, however, his daughter Ghislaine told *Hello!*, the celebrity magazine, 'There was no evidence of suicide or a heart attack. I think he was murdered. My father was not perfect, but he never committed suicide.'

Subsequent investigations, apparently supported by a number of FBI documents, allege that the tycoon had links to organised crime in the Balkans and that he worked for Mossad, the feared Israeli intelligence service.

According to one theory, Maxwell had threatened Mossad that, unless they paid him $400 million, he would expose his secret dealings with them. Instead of providing the money, a small group of Mossad officers set about planning his murder. They knew that he was gradually becoming mentally unstable and paranoid. He was taking a cocktail of drugs – Halcion and Zanax – which had serious side effects.

The group of Mossad plotters sensed he could cause incalculable harm to Israel and a plan to kill him was prepared in the utmost secrecy. A four-man squad was briefed.

Then Maxwell was contacted. He was told to fly to Gibraltar, go aboard the *Lady Ghislaine* and sail to the Canary Islands. There, at sea, he would receive his $400 million 'quick fix' in the form of a banker's draft. Maxwell did as he was told. On the night of 4 November 1991, the *Lady Ghislaine* was at sea. Unknown to its crew, the death squad had cast an electronic net over the yacht to block all radio transmissions. The security cameras on board had been switched off. After midnight there were only two men on the bridge; 120ft (6.1m) behind them, Maxwell appeared on deck. He had been instructed to do so in a previous message from Mossad.

A small boat came alongside. On board were four black-suited men. Three scrambled onto the yacht. In a second, it was all over. Two held Maxwell. The third plunged a syringe into his neck behind his ear. A measured dose of nerve agent was injected. Robert Maxwell was immobilised. He was lowered off the deck into the water.

As Victor Ostrovsky, a former Mossad agent, later said, 'On that cold night Mossad's problems with Robert Maxwell were over.'

# ANT ON DECK
## SOUTH AFRICA, 1992

Anthony Steward had become bored with regular sailing and, while he was sailing double-handed around Cape Horn, ideas started to formulate in his mind on the ultimate sailing challenge, the only sailing feat that had not yet been accomplished: circumnavigation of the world in an open boat.

Ant sold everything that he owned. He cut corners and scrounged wherever he could, even talking a friend into letting him build his small craft inside the latter's apartment!

When he eventually set off from Cape Town in early 1992, many expected never to see him again. Almost the last thing he told well-wishers before setting off was that he had a hereditary disease, which he controlled by steroids. It could incapacitate him very quickly and could kill him if left untreated.

His journey would be an eventful one. Five days out of Cape Town, his boat, *NCS Challenger*, capsized, then righted herself immediately, and took off at speed with Ant in the water, luckily attached by a harness line. That was to be the first of many capsizes, so many that Ant has no idea of the number for the whole voyage.

Between Cape Town and St Helena he lost his navigation tables in a capsize and lost two days while drifting uncontrolled after being incapacitated by food poisoning through eating raw fish. On the next leg he damaged his sextant and, as a result, sailed 50 miles (80.5km) past Ascension Island before seeing gannets flying across his route and following them in.

The leg from the Caribbean to Panama he found to be particularly tough. He nearly lost his rig when the upper pin came out of his forestay soon after he had left St Maarten and then was capsized repeatedly in a gale, which produced large breaking seas and left him totally spent.

He then sailed to Bora Bora via the Galapagos and the Marquesas, loosening keel bolts in a collision with a floating tree en route. After leaving American Samoa he was demasted in a squall when the cap shroud parted. He retrieved all the bits and pieces, then went back in for repairs. Feeling that he could not afford the three-week delay waiting for a new mast, he tied the broken mast on deck like a giant jousting pole and set off again. From Brisbane, Ant harbour-hopped around the top of Australia to Darwin. Though warned of potential problems rounding Fraser Island just north of Darwin, he ran aground hard on a sandbank, damaging the keel and opening a leak, which was to plague him later.

It was after Christmas Island, however, that he was tested almost beyond his limits. On 13 July 1992 he was sailing through a storm and had the hatches open while attempting to talk to Cape Town Radio. A large breaking wave knocked *NCS Challenger* down and she flooded through the open hatches, destroying all the electronics. In her flooded and unstable condition, Ant could not right her for half an hour, during which time the self-steering gear was destroyed and the mast bent.

He had to cut the rig away to prevent further capsize and spent the night sorting out the mess and bailing. With the wind continuing to blow at 30–40 knots (55.6–74.1km/h) for four days, he covered 240 miles (386km) with no sail. After the storm he spotted an island and headed towards it, realising too late that there was an outer reef, which he could not avoid. The boat was washed across the reef by the surf, with Ant just hanging on in the cockpit while the hull rolled over and over, taking a hammering and coming off the other side minus keel and rudder.

Ant now found that his little life raft had, for its own reasons, given up the ghost and would not stay inflated. He left his boat stranded on a reef while he, bleeding from his ordeal, set off across the lagoon for the island some 750 yards (686m) away. He found himself surrounded by sharks. With only a knife and marlinespike to defend himself, he swam that distance slashing at the sharks all the way to the beach.

On the deserted Cerf Island he found a derelict fisherman's cottage but no fresh water, so he lived on pawpaws and coconuts for the next nine days until he was rescued by a fishing boat, which he'd attracted with a flare. In the interim, *NCS Challenger* had washed up on the beach with the hull surprisingly intact.

Ant was taken to another island by the fisherman, where he was admitted into hospital and stayed for a week. While he was there, the fishermen returned to Cerf Island and took *NCS Challenger* in tow to Mahe. From there she was shipped back to South Africa, where Ant repaired her while on honeymoon with his new wife, Sue.

When he eventually left East London in the Eastern Cape, he suffered an attack of his disease because he had forgotten to take his medication, an omission that resulted in his being rushed to hospital on arrival at Port Elizabeth, his own home port.

After his release, he still had to make it around Cape Agulhas and the Cape of Good Hope before reaching Cape Town, his point of departure. His arrival in Cape Town saw a turnout of boats of all types and sizes, from dinghies to a harbour tug spraying its water cannon. Thousands of people lined the Victoria and Alfred Waterfront and he sailed in amid incredible noise to a great welcome. At the quayside, *NCS Challenger* was lifted out by crane, with Ant and Sue still on board, and lowered onto the hard to meet the media.

It had taken over two years, but, unrepentant, he began making preparations for his next madman's trip, to sail nonstop around the world in a 20ft (6.1m) boat, this one with a cabin!

However, he never made the trip and today is chief of Global Operations for The Moorings, one of the world's premier yacht charter companies.

# THE TRAGIC LOUISE LONGO

## BAY OF BISCAY, 1994

In 1994 Louise Longo, a French woman of Sicilian origin, embarked on a voyage in rather unusual circumstances that would eventually end in tragedy.

She agreed to join Bernard, her ex-husband, on a three-week voyage from Rochefort to Senegal on the sailboat *Jan van Gent*.

They had separated after 13 years of marriage two years previously, and he had since spiralled further down into drink and depression. They had a five-year-old daughter, Gaella, and it was for her sake that they had arranged the trip all together, despite Louise's private misgivings.

On 5 October, six days into their voyage, a storm blew up in the Bay of Biscay. Two giant waves lashed at the boat and fearing a third one – but against all reason – Bernard insisted that they abandon ship and take to a small life raft.

After much pleading against this on Louise's part, she acquiesced under Bernard's assurance that the raft was well equipped with all the necessities: fishing tackle, food, water, flares, matches and a first-aid kit.

In the event, the raft was equipped with none of these things except wet flares and matches – caused by a leak! Louise had grabbed a bottle of water, however, while Bernard had taken only cigarettes and rum.

They were cold and hungry, wet and thirsty, as they watched their sailing boat drift away on the waves. Over the next few days their situation worsened. Bernard became considerably weaker and, after they had decided to drink tiny amounts of seawater, he became delirious.

Louise managed to calm him and eventually he fell asleep – and died. Ironically, it started to rain later that day. She tried to explain to Gaella what had happened, but three days later she had to undergo the ordeal of putting Bernard's body into the water.

Louise and Gaella, exhausted physically and mentally, struggled on, baling water out, buffeted by sharks and beyond feeling either fear or hope. A couple of days later the unimaginable happened. A Russian freighter spotted them and spent six hours fighting the swell to get close enough to pick them up. This proved impossible.

The crew, however, called for a helicopter to pick them up. Louise and Gaella had no inking of this, however, and, within a few hours, Gaella died.

With no emotional resources left, Louise put the small emaciated body into the water and prepared to jump in herself. At that very same moment, the helicopter arrived and picked her up.

Perhaps the worst ordeal was now to come: she was treated with contempt by those medical people charged with looking after her as the press started to hint that perhaps she was a murderer! An even more horrible irony was that, a day or so later, the *Jan van Gent* was found safe and sound, unharmed by the storm.

# HELP US OR WE'LL DIE!
## QUEENSLAND, AUSTRALIA, 1998

It's a diver's worst nightmare: miles from shore, you surface to find your charter boat nowhere in sight. You call for help, but there's no response. There are no outcroppings to hold on to. You hope that someone realises their mistake before it's too late.

This is what presumably happened to Eileen and Tom Lonergan on 25 January 1998, at St Crispin's Reef, a popular dive site on the Great Barrier Reef, 25 miles (40.2km) off the coast of Queensland, Australia.

On the fateful day, they had gone out with the Queensland-based Port Douglas scuba boat *Outer Edge*. The couple did three dives in the area before being given permission to dive on their own. Other divers reported seeing them climb back on board for the return trip, but then disappear into the water again.

Stories vary, but, at the end of the day, the crew did a head count and came up with only 24 of their 26 clients. Someone pointed out two young divers who had jumped in to swim off the bow, and the crew, assuming that they had missed them, adjusted the count to 26. With the swimmers on board, the *Outer Edge* headed back to port.

Two days later, Geoffrey Nairn, the boat's skipper, discovered Eileen and Tom's personal belongings in the *Outer Edge*'s lost-property bin, including Tom's wallet, glasses and clothes. Concerned, he called the owner of the

Gone Walkabout Hostel in Cairns, where the couple had been staying, to see if they had returned. They had not. A five-day search began, which turned up no trace of Eileen or Tom. After more than 48 hours in the ocean, the couple could have drowned, or been eaten by sharks. But as the chilling story broke, other theories emerged.

One was that they had committed suicide, or a murder-suicide had taken place. Journals in their hotel room hinted at personal troubles, but the couple were devout Catholics with good prospects. Relatives angrily discounted the theory. Tom's mother Elizabeth reckoned they were left behind, that someone had left them in the water and did not report it for two and a half days.

Another scenario had the Lonergans using the dive boat as part of an elaborate hoax to fake their deaths. Jeanette Brenthall, owner of a bookshop in Port Douglas, believes the couple came into her store on 27 January, two days after their dive trip. The pair were also reportedly sighted in a hotel in downtown Darwin.

Reports of a boat less than 1 mile (1.6km) from St Crispin's Reef seem to support theories that the couple had been picked up. But the Lonergans' bank accounts were never touched, and no one ever collected on their insurance policies. A few weeks after they'd gone missing, some of their personal dive gear washed up on a beach 75 miles (121km) from the dive site.

Few people in Port Douglas – and certainly not those who know the Barrier Reef well – are happy with the official version of events.

While the authorities initially claimed that the couple had drowned or were eaten by tiger sharks, diving experts say that they could have easily swum to a well-frequented pontoon and waited to be picked up by rescuers.

Grahame Connett, a local diver, said, 'There was a Quicksilver dive site – a brightly lit permanent platform in the ocean used by divers – that is 2.7 nautical miles [5km] from the dive site. It was in the area, if they wanted to go there. There were three or four boats in the area and a dive platform, and they [the Lonergans] had five hours of light available. There's no doubt that they could have reached one of those. Conditions were excellent.'

Like others, Mr Connett says that it seems strange that so much of the Lonergans' personal equipment – diving vests, weights, tanks, weight belts and two cameras – was recovered from the sea but with no trace of their bodies. And, if they were attacked by sharks, why wasn't their clothing shredded and bloodied?

Six months later, a weathered dive slate – a device used to communicate underwater – with contact information for Eileen's father was found floating in the same vicinity as the gear, bearing the words, 'Please help us or we will die. January 26, 8:00a.m.'

# 'CAPTAIN CALAMITY' STRIKES (YET) AGAIN

## IRISH SEA, 2000

On Thursday, 10 August 2000, Holyhead coastguards off North Wales, picking up a call for assistance, observed a small yacht called *Plus VAT* travelling up the estuary. Both the all-weather and inshore boats were then launched but, before either could reach it, *Plus VAT* ran aground. An attempt to tow the vessel was then made and, after the line broke, it was eventually berthed in Rhyl Harbour.

It was the twelfth time its owner and constructor, Eric Abbott, had called for assistance in one year – and twice in one day! Exasperated coastguards began investigating whether they could take action against him.

Abbott had begun building his 24ft (7.3m) yacht 18 years previously, when he lost his job as a painter and decorator. He first set sail from Rhyl, North Wales, in July 1999, blaming both Margaret Thatcher and Chancellor Gordon Brown for forcing him out to sea. The name *Plus VAT* was a protest against tax.

Abbott, who said he enjoyed going out to sea alone to 'find himself', had no official navigation system on his boat and used only a 1997 copy of the AA Road Atlas to sail across the Irish Sea. Although admitting on several occasions that he didn't know where he was, he denied he was irresponsible – such accusations were 'absolute rubbish', he told reporters. 'When you are out there on your own, the Irish Sea can be quite a big place. I have one map but it isn't that detailed.'

Despite the fact that his adventures have cost the coastguard service up to £55,000, he vowed to continue and shouted to journalists through his cabin door, 'I'm not giving up,' adding, 'Bring out the champagne!' Asked whether he had a coastal skipper's licence, Abbott shouted, 'I don't need one, I'm far more intelligent.'

After some pleading, the Maritime and Coastguard Agency persuaded him to undergo a free ten-day sea skipper course run by the Royal Yachting Association, which normally costs just £500.

A year later, Captain Calamity, as the press had now dubbed him, hinted that he was thinking of trying again.

'The Channel Islands look quite appealing. It's pretty far to sail, but I could put the yacht on a trailer and take it to the south coast, although it could be expensive down there.'

# SCRAPCRAFT

## NEW YORK, USA, 2000

David Pearlman – or Poppa Neutrino, as the 65-year-old jazz musician of the funky jazz band the Flying Neutrinos Family Band likes to be called – along with his wife and two colleagues left Fermeuse, Newfoundland, on 15 June 1998 bound for France aboard a 26ft (7.9m) raft called *Son of Town Hall* made from plywood, plastic bottles, netting and other materials salvaged from New York streets and scrapyards.

Also on board were two Rottweiler dogs named Thor and Siegfried, and a small mutt called Willie. The crew had left New York City in June 1997 on the transatlantic portion of their voyage, but had to put into Fermeuse because they were running short of food. After coping with periods of little wind on the Grand Banks, as well as a severe mid-Atlantic storm, the voyagers decided to head the raft for Ireland rather than France, and arrived on 13 August.

An earlier raft, *Town Hall*, had been built between 1988 and 1990 in Provincetown, Massachusetts, from a condemned barge, discarded floating docks and driftwood from the beach. Powered by a set of paddlewheels driven by a recycled generator motor from Provincetown's Town Hall – hence the raft's name – it had served as the travelling home and stage for the Neutrinos as they travelled from Massachusetts to New York City, arriving in August 1991.

Here it remained anchored at Pier 25 in the Hudson River

in Manhattan, within sight of the World Trade Center, the home base for all the Neutrinos. It was also here that the *Son of Town Hall* was built, incorporating pieces from the *Town Hall* for continuity.

Basically, *Son of Town Hall* was a plywood box with three cabins that sat on top of a long base. The raft was made buoyant by polystyrene with a 20-horsepower diesel engine to get it in and out of port, three masts and sails, a life-raft, radar, electricity generator and a global positioning system (GPS).

The Neutrinos' biggest problem had been getting the raft to steer downwind. With a flat bottom, and drawing only 2in (50.8cm), there was no resistance underwater. Every time the wind went over 15 knots (27.8km/h), the raft would turn sideways. After years of testing and redesigning, they finally solved the problem by installing a huge retractable dagger board at the stern, just ahead of the rudder. This, together with a very small storm square sail hoisted at the bow, effectively turned the raft downwind under all circumstances.

After the *Son of Town Hall* left New York in 1997, the *Town Hall* continued to serve as rehearsal, relaxation and living space for the younger generation of Neutrinos, and other artists and musicians. However, on 8 May 2000, suddenly and without warning, an unknown towing company, under orders from the Hudson River Park Trust, arrived at Pier 25 and summarily towed away the rafts *Town Hall* and *Child of Amazon*. After being towed up the Hudson River to Pier 40, the *Child* was loaded onto a barge to be taken to an undisclosed destination. In the attempt to lift the *Town Hall*, presumably to do the same with it, the straps broke, and the raft fell to the water, breaking into many pieces. The owner of the *Child*, Balasz, who had lived on board for several years, was refused the right to go aboard and collect his personal belongings. He lost, among much else, his green card and papers, the ashes of his father, and his cat, who was on board and has not been found since.

Poppa Neutrino said, 'How ironic that this symbol of creative recycling, which never, despite the accusations of its enemies, created any pollution anywhere it went, instead gathering and transforming into working art, the debris of an over-industrialised society, should end up as a clean-up incident caused by the euphemistically titled "Hudson River Park Trust".'

In 2008 Poppa Neutrino moved to Burlington, on Vermont's Lake Champlain and in 2010 was planning a circumnavigation of the globe with three companions and three dogs aboard a new craft. However, on 9 November they were driven onto rocks and had to be rescued. 'The vessel was everything I wanted it to be,' Poppa told newsmen. 'I told the Coast Guard people it was unsinkable. They said, "Never say that." They were right. Anything will break up if it's been smashing into a wall for two and a half hours.'

Neutrino died of heart failure on 23 January 2011, in a hospital in New Orleans, Louisiana. His life was celebrated at a jazz funeral in New Orleans attended by dozens of friends and relatives wearing bright costumes.

# OVERBOARD AT THE HORN!
## CAPE HORN, 2003

Sixty-year-old John J. Curtin, of Old Lyme, Connecticut, took early retirement from a career as a trust and estate settlement officer to pursue his dream of extended blue-water sailing and rounding Cape Horn. In *Queequeg III*, he and six others departed Mobile, Alabama, on 17 October 2002, on a 16,000 mile (25,749km) west-to-east circumnavigation of South America.

The owner and skipper of *Queequeg* – a Morgan 462 centre-cockpit cutter-rigged ketch – was Quen Cultra, a 63-year-old licensed captain and global circumnavigator with more than 30 years' experience and 35,000 miles (56,326km) of offshore sailing experience.

Although it was 9p.m. as they approached Cape Horn on the night of 7 February 2003, it was still light in the southern hemisphere. John was on watch, and the first mate was at the helm. Everyone else was below.

The seas were forbidding – mountainous walls of water estimated at 30–40ft (9.1–12.2m), with curling, cresting, foaming tops. At times the seas were extremely confused and the sky was mean and ugly.

They'd been working their way through stormy conditions for about 18 hours, when barometric pressure fell rapidly. Quen figured they were in for a good blow – and he was right.

*Queequeg* was running under a very small foresail, surfing down waves at 15–18 knots (27.8–33.3km/h), but under control. It was wild and exhilarating, sailing on the edge as John later termed it, and he was loving every moment of it. The first mate had relieved him from his final hour at the helm and he sat under the canvas dodger facing aft on the port or windward side of the vessel. As he looked up at the sky, he remembered seeing a small patch of blue and told the first mate that perhaps it meant a break in the miserable weather of the past few days.

He then turned to look over his right shoulder when – wham! – a large breaking wave hit *Queequeg* broadside on the port side. John later said it was as if a train had struck. He was swept immediately from port to starboard, and thrust through the plastic window panel of the dodger into waters of only 40–45°F. *Queequeg* was rolled over on her side and the mast struck the water. In seconds John could feel the cold seawater enter his boots and foul-weather gear. Five, six, seven seconds went by.

Then he felt a tug, and knew immediately that his tether connecting him to *Queequeg* had not failed. Not yet, anyway.

When he surfaced he could see the mast beginning to rise so he pulled on his tether, grabbed a lifeline and, as *Queequeg* began to lift herself upright, used the momentum to roll himself into the flooded cockpit.

The first mate, who had been knocked down, avoided being swept into the ocean by grabbing the helm with the proverbial death grip. Prior to the knockdown they knew that, if they lost someone over the side in such conditions, it would be difficult – if not impossible – to retrieve them. That was understood among the crew.

The canvas cockpit and protective screen had been crushed and the stainless-steel framework tubing bent and distorted. The small foresail had been ripped and shredded like tissue paper. Below deck, all equipment and supplies not secured had been thrown from port to starboard. John's bunkmate in the aft cabin had been trapped for a few moments under the bedboard, mattress and other debris.

Quen pulled on his foul-weather gear, helped pull his daughter, Ashley, out of a pile of canned goods and other items, and hurried on deck to survey the scene.

John and the first mate furled the shredded jib the best they could, and proceeded to raise the stormsail to give *Queequeg* some directional stability to continue their easterly course around the Horn. They rounded the Horn at 1.15p.m. the next day, about 12 miles (19.3km) offshore.

Captain Quen then decided to deploy the Para-Tech sea anchor, a parachute-type device some 18ft (5.5m) in diameter designed to hold the bow to the seas, and dampen boat speed and motion. Deploying the sea anchor was tricky, in that the manoeuvre required turning *Queequeg* about into the large seas. At just the right moment, when there was some relatively flat water between the steep, breaking waves, John was able to turn the ketch about so the captain and first mate could successfully set the sea anchor. The device worked perfectly, despite the best efforts of Mother Nature, who hammered them for another 12 hours with large seas and gale-force winds. It turned out that they had been slammed by three low-pressure systems in succession.

In the early-morning hours of the next day, they were greeted by relative calm. The gale had broken. The winds had subsided to about 20 knots (37km/h) and the seas had diminished in size. They quickly retrieved the sea anchor and set course for the Falkland Islands, some 400 miles (644km) away.

Paul Quentin 'Quen' Cultra, lifelong sailor and adventurer, enjoyed his last sunrise at sea on 20 January 2009, in the Indian Ocean off the coast of Madagascar.

# ROW, ROW, ROW YOUR BOAT!

## NEW ZEALAND, 2003

In 2000–1, 57-year-old Jim Shekhdar made the first solo and unaided Pacific Ocean row from Peru to Australia.

His boat was only 23ft (7m) long and just under 7ft (2.1m) at its widest point with a 7ft (2.1m) long cabin at the back, in which he slept. He couldn't sit up in it, but could lie down in it, and it contained all his radio communications. There was also a middle section containing a sliding seat for rowing, and there was a little section at the front with a waterproof hatch used for storage.

In the tradition of great but eccentric travellers, his journey started badly: he was refused permission to set off from Chile; when he departed from Peru, he realised he had set off without a tin opener; then he ran out of cooking gas.

On his incredible journey, Shekhdar braved 50ft (15.2m) waves, nearly collided with an oil tanker and was repeatedly head-butted by an 11ft (3.3m) white pointer shark. He made friends with a school of tuna, which shadowed him the entire 10,000 miles (16,093km).

Shekhdar never slept for more than 90 minutes at a time. He'd rationed 6,000 calories a day, but the voyage he'd expected to take five months lasted nine; by the end, he had lost 60lb (27.2kg) pounds and was living on cold pasta soaked in desalinated seawater.

After 274 days at sea, the Briton who became the first

person to row the Pacific unassisted was forced to swim the last 30 or so yards (27.4m) when his boat capsized.

Not content with his Pacific success, he then sought the impossible – a joint crossing of the South Pacific and the South Atlantic oceans, from New Zealand to South Africa. Traversing the most difficult waters in the world, with a rounding of the legendary Cape Horn, was his last quest.

On 5 November 2003, he left Invercargill in his specially designed rowing boat, *Hornette*, and after just 13 days had travelled nearly 750 miles (1,207km) through some of the most hostile seas in the world. On 18 November, however, a storm gusting over 100 knots (185km/h) with huge confused seas caused *Hornette* to pitch-pole, destroying almost all deck gear and generating equipment plus putting a hole in Jim's head as he careered into a hatch.

Continuing was not an option, so he reluctantly called for assistance and had to be rescued.

The National Institute of Water and Atmospheric Research, which diverted one of its ships to rescue the rower, then impounded his boat to defray the cost of the rescue. (The flight of the Orion spotter plane that guided the rescue ship to Shekhdar cost US$64,500.)

Shekhdar remained defiant, however. The one-time management consultant from Leamington Spa in Warwickshire claimed his boat wasn't 'salvage', as it hadn't been abandoned and was still seaworthy. He was planning to have it shipped back to Britain. 'Obviously, there's a cost to do a rescue like this, but you can't squeeze blood out of a stone,' he said.

# THE ECOLOGICAL
## *MERMAID*

### JAPAN, 2008

Kenichi Horie has been a folk hero in Japan since 1962, when, in a 19ft (5.8m) boat, he became the first person to sail solo across the Pacific. At the time the Japanese government discouraged overseas travel and refused him a passport, so Horie set sail under cover of darkness and arrived in San Francisco 94 days later on the first *Mermaid* – unannounced with no passport, no money, no English and no idea what to do next.

He was befriended by a local boater and brought into a marina, but nobody knew quite what to do about him politically. The Second World War was still fresh in the American psyche, and, legally, he should have been repatriated immediately.

However, San Francisco's mayor, George Christopher, called the former president Dwight Eisenhower, on whose staff Christopher had served, for advice. Eisenhower said that the mayor should do what was right, for Japan and for young people. So Christopher welcomed the young seafarer with open arms, awarding him the key to the city and a special 30-day visa.

That voyage – and San Francisco's warm welcome – hit papers nationwide, catapulting the then unknown Horie to cult hero status and, reportedly, helping to 'open up' Japan, which started issuing passports for the first time the following year.

In the succeeding years Horie logged seven more solo voyages, including circumnavigating the globe both latitudinally and longitudinally and piloting a 9ft (2.7m) sailboat from San Francisco to Okinawa.

In 1989 he sailed from San Francisco to Nishinomiya on the smallest open sea yacht – 9ft (2.7m) in length overall.

In 1996 he solo-sailed a solar-powered vessel, *Malt's Mermaid*, a 31ft (9.4m) craft partly made from 22,000 recycled aluminium cans, from Ecuador to Tokyo without stopping.

For the most part, the trip was problem-free, though he confessed to making one crucial miscalculation. 'The trip would have been better if I had brought more beer.'

Two days into his four-and-a-half-month trip on *Malt's Mermaid*, one of his water purifiers conked out. Fearing a failure in his backup system, Horie shifted into beer-conservation mode so that he'd have at least one form of potable liquid to sustain him through the journey.

In 1999, with sponsorship from one of Japan's major breweries, Suntory, Horie's boat, *Malt's Mermaid II* – a 32⅘ft (10m) long, 17⅖ft (5.3m) wide catamaran, constructed from five rows of small stainless-steel beer kegs (528, in all) welded together end to end to form the sides of the two hulls – sailed from San Francisco to the Akashi Channel Bridge, Japan. To make further use of recycled materials, the vessel's junk-rigged, full-batten sails, trampolines and other canvas gear were manufactured from reprocessed plastic bottles.

The year 2002 marked the fortieth anniversary of his 'Alone on the Pacific' voyage, and Horie sailed the same course as the 1962 voyage to show his appreciation to the city of San Francisco. *Malt's Mermaid III* was a restored version of the 19ft (5.8m) *Mermaid* he used for his first trip.

On 16 March 2008, the then 69-year-old Japanese sailor left the Hawaii Yacht Club, Honolulu, in the *Suntory Mermaid II*, bound for Japan. He arrived on 4 July 2008 in the Kii Channel offshore of Hinomisaki Cape, Wakayama, Japan, having made the world's longest solo voyage in a wave-powered boat using green technology.

*Suntory Mermaid II* was powered by a single solar battery and made from recycled materials. Horie said: 'Throughout history, mankind has used wind for power, but no one has appeared to be serious about wave power. I think I'm a lucky boy as this wave power system has remained virtually untouched.'

Horie says his voyages are aimed at inspiring young people as well as bringing attention to the environment and the importance of recycling. With all his open-ocean experience, Horie is well prepared for the rigours of isolation, but still finds the starkness of his environment unsettling. 'Everywhere I look there is horizon – nothing but horizon,' he says. 'I feel like an astronaut in space.'

# 'MIRACLE MAN
# OF THE PACIFIC'

## PACIFIC OCEAN, 2014

On 30 January 2014, on Tile Islet, a small part of Ebon Atoll in the Marshall Islands, two locals, Amy Libokmeto and Russell Laikedrik, found a Salvadorian man José Salvador Alvarenga, naked, clutching a knife and shouting in Spanish. He was treated in a hospital in Majuro before flying to his family home in El Salvador on 10 February, and from there the first words of his incredible story were relayed to a disbelieving world. Alvarenga claimed he'd spent the last 13 months drifting in a fishing boat 6,500 miles (10,460km) across the Pacific from Mexico. In doing so he'd become the first person in history to survive in a small boat lost at sea for more than a year.

But there were doubts. His condition and strength surprised local doctors, who were used to treating fishermen who drift ashore after weeks or even months at sea that were emaciated and fragile. Alvarenga's only serious pain was in his joints, while his skin was hardly cracked or burned. What's more, his account sometimes appeared unclear and he mixed up details, such as the date of his departure from Mexico and his age, as well as that of his companion, Ezekiel – who had not survived.

Fishing boat owner Villermino Rodriguez Jose Manuel Aragon said, 'There are things that don't match up. I knew him, but I have a lot of doubts.' Fisherman Belarmino Rodriguez Solis told an El Salvador newspaper, 'It's a great surprise. Nobody survives more than two or three months in those conditions. We even laid flowers in the palm hut where he lived.' Another fisherman said, 'We're surprised, we couldn't believe it.'

Jack Niedenthal, on the other hand, a film-maker based on Majuro, said, 'He got off the boat with a very bushy beard. He's having trouble walking, his legs are very skinny. I'm not ready to call this a hoax, I think this guy has done some serious time at sea.'

Erik van Sebille, a Sydney-based oceanographer at the University of New South Wales, said there was a good chance a boat drifting off Mexico's west coast would eventually be carried by currents to the Marshall Islands. Such a journey would typically take 18 months to two years depending on the winds and currents, although 13 months was possible. He added that experts had measured the Pacific currents by tracking mounds of rubbish floating across the ocean – and said Mr Alvarenga was lucky to have hit the Marshalls when he did. If he hadn't, he would probably have ended up floating into a giant floating garbage patch estimated to be the size of Western Australia.

Alvarenga's own story was that several hours into his fateful fishing trip, he and his 22-year-old companion Ezekiel Cordoba were engulfed in a storm and he radioed for help. 'He said the engine had broken on the boat and he sounded desperate,' recalled Hector Arebalo Castellonos, who was monitoring communications. Another fisherman recalled Mr Alvarenga cursing the broken engine over the radio. They were the last words his friends heard from him. His was one of three boats lost at sea that day.

Alvarenga and Ezekiel then drifted, surviving on turtles, fish and seabirds caught with their bare hands, which they ate raw, drinking their blood when there was no rain and, when that wasn't available, their own urine. About four months into their journey, however, Ezekiel, weakened and depressed, lost hope. 'There was enough food, but he wouldn't eat it,' said Mr Alvarenga. 'He was getting skinnier and skinnier. He just sat on the other side of the boat and decided to pass away.'

One morning, Ezekiel told his older shipmate he believed he was almost gone. Alvarenga told him not to think about it and to take a nap. He held a water bottle to his young friend's lips but he could not swallow. And then, 'he was gone'. They had been at sea for four months. Alvarenga, terrified of being alone, kept the boy's corpse on board at first, talking to it. It was six days before he decided he could no longer keep chatting to a dead man. 'First I washed his feet. His clothes were useful, so I stripped off a pair of shorts and a sweatshirt. I put that on – it was red, with little skull-and-crossbones – and then I dumped him in. And as I slid him into the water, I fainted.'

Alvarenga claimed that before Cordoba's death, the younger man had made him promise not to eat his corpse and to visit his mother. Two months after making landfall, he travelled from El Salvador to Mexico to see Cordoba's mother, Ana Rosa Diaz. The pair cried and hugged and Alvarenga spent two hours answering her questions. 'I would have liked to have welcomed my son like this,' said Mrs Diaz afterwards. 'I feel better now. I am more at peace because I know what happened. Now I know what my son's last words were.'

In April 2014 Alvarenga was subjected to a psychological examination and lie-detector test by a US law firm which declared that his story was '100 per cent real'.

There ensued a bidding war for the rights to Alvarenga's memoir. The resulting book, *438 Days – An Incredible True Story of Survival at Sea*, saw Ezekiel Cordoba's relatives change their attitude. In December 2015 the Cordoba family accused Alvarenga of turning cannibal to survive. They were now suing the Salvadorian fisherman for $1m for eating their relative!

Alvarenga's lawyer said, 'I believe that this demand is part of the pressure from this family to divide the proceeds of the book royalties. Many believe the book is making my client a rich man, but what he will earn is much less than people think.'

Alvarenga said he had wanted to take his own life when Ezekiel died. 'For four days I wanted to kill myself. But I couldn't feel the desire – I didn't want to feel the pain. I couldn't do it. I had my mind on God. If I was going to die, I would be with God. So I wasn't scared ... I imagine this is an incredible story for people.'